The Art of Managing

The Art of Managing

How to Assess and Perfect Your Management Style

Cabot L. Jaffee

Fredric D. Frank

Michael R. Struth

Cabot L. Jaffee, Jr.

Addison-Wesley Publishing Company, Inc.
Reading, Massachusetts   Menlo Park, California   New York
Don Mills, Ontario   Wokingham, England   Amsterdam
Bonn   Sydney   Singapore   Tokyo   Madrid   San Juan

The publisher offers discounts on this book when ordered in quantity for special sales. For more information please contact:
Corporate & Professional Publishing Group
Addison-Wesley Publishing Company, Inc.
One Jacob Way
Reading, Massachusetts 01867

Library of Congress Cataloging-in-Publication Data

The Art of managing : how to assess and perfect your man-
    agement style / Cabot L. Jaffee . . . [et al.].
        p.   cm.
    ISBN 0-201-18200-9 (pbk.)
    1. Management.   I. Jaffee, Cabot L., 1936–
HD38.A73   1991
658.4'09—dc20   90-25815
                                                     CIP

Cover design by Richard Rossiter
Text design by Joyce C. Weston
Set in 11 point Sabon by DEKR Corporation, Woburn, MA

ISBN 0-201-18200-9

Printed on recycled and acid-free paper

1   2   3   4   5-MW-9594939291

First Printing, June 1991

To our families and parents for providing
the coaching, counseling, and support
that enabled us to write this book.

Contents

Preface

THIS book has four audiences: those of you who are presently managers/supervisors; those of you who wish to become managers/supervisors; those of you who are just thinking about it; and those of you who are not in a formal sense managers/supervisors, but feel you need to apply managerial/supervisory attributes in other areas of your life.

We designed this book with a dual purpose in mind: to allow you to test yourself on both your overall managerial capability, or Managerial Quotient (MQ), and your MQ's components or attributes (mq's), for a better understanding of your relative strengths and weaknesses; and, to start you off on the road to further self-development.

The tests, for the most part, involve situations that either simulate or resemble frequently encountered managerial/supervisory challenges in realistic organizational settings. We think you will find them interesting. Becoming involved in the situations and putting a reasonable amount of effort into completing the tests will provide you with accurate, meaningful feedback on your MQ and on your specific attributes, or mq's, of managerial/supervisory capability.

To begin, we provide specific suggestions on the mq's of managerial/supervisory capability. By the end of the book, you will have worked out a developmental plan to enhance various attributes. As you progress through the book you will gain a better overall understanding of yourself, as well as specific techniques for self-development.

What you will discover is your *Managerial Quotient,* or *MQ.* As opposed to mq, MQ reflects one's *overall* capability as a manager/ supervisor. In small letters, mq refers to the individual components of the MQ. There are seven mq's. These are the Administrator, the Analyzer, the Counselor, the Communicator, the Meeter, the Mentor, and the Aspirer. Tests are provided for each of these seven attributes. We then explore in depth an eighth component that is also associated with managerial/supervisory success—the Self-Developer.

Many of the ideas in this book were developed during the 20 years that we have been involved in the development and implementation of selection strategies, tests, and developmental programs for literally hundreds of organizations of all types and sizes, both in the private and public sectors and in the United States and abroad. During that time many people contributed to the thinking, and to the refinement, of our ideas. We would like to thank all the managers and supervisors from our client organizations who have given us additional insight and have helped make this book possible.

On a final note, we have attempted to write a useful book, one that will allow people to evaluate and develop their managerial/supervisory attributes in interesting and meaningful ways. The Administrator, the Analyzer, the Counselor, the Communicator, the Meeter, the Mentor, the Aspirer, and the Self-Developer are inside all of us, waiting to emerge once we unlock the doors. Our hope is that this book will be the key.

Cabot L. Jaffee
Fredric D. Frank
Michael R. Struth
Cabot L. Jaffee, Jr.

June, 1991

The Art of Managing

CHAPTER 1

Managerial Roles

MANY people have attempted to develop explanations of what contributes to managerial and supervisory success. For the most part, and with different degrees of emphasis, these explanations have included people skills, communication skills, analyzing and decision-making skills, and organizing and controlling skills as contributory factors. Typically complementing these are desire for success and a willingness to work toward developing oneself to the fullest extent possible.

Basing our decisions on almost 40 years of collective research and experience with virtually all types of organizations, we have selected eight basic attributes that we believe are associated with managerial and supervisory success. These, to a large extent, parallel those that others have selected, but there are some differences. Our eight basic attributes are divided into two categories: one that comprises competency factors and one that comprises attitudinal factors. Competency factors involve the exercising of skills and abilities. This category includes the Administrator, the Analyzer, the Counselor, the Communicator, and the Meeter. Attitudinal factors are associated with wants, desires, and needs. This category includes the three remaining attributes: the Mentor, the Aspirer, and the Self-Developer.

We will define these attributes later on. Here it is important to note that each attribute label, for example, the Administrator, has been chosen because it most clearly conveys the real meaning of the elements associated with the particular attribute. It may seem that some attributes are missing from our list. For example, one might ask, where is the leader, or the negotiator? These are certainly words we hear quite often; to us, however, they are either too broad (such as the leader), or they are already included on our list, subsumed under another attribute (such as the negotiator). More specifically, *leader* encompasses most, if not all, of our eight attributes; therefore, it is not that useful a term in trying to determine what makes a good manager or supervisor. The term *negotiator*, meaning one who can negotiate successfully, relates to the proper application of the attributes of the Administrator, the Analyzer, the Meeter, and the Communicator, complemented by the Aspirer.

In summary, then, we believe we have included all of the necessary ingredients for being a successful manager or supervisor. Our eight attributes are those necessary ingredients.

As you will see, we have developed independent measures for the seven attributes of the Administrator, the Analyzer, the Counselor, the Communicator, the Meeter, the Mentor, and the Aspirer. These tests came about as a result of many years of research and experience in designing instruments for the selection of managers and supervisors at all organizational levels within both the private and public sectors. With regard to the Self-Developer, we have provided numerous tips (approximately 400 suggestions in Chapter 9) on how you can improve your attributes and be an active Self-Developer.

For the most part, the tests in Chapters 2 through 8, those that focus on the first seven attributes, necessarily differ from one another in type and content because the attributes are different from one another. Also, the tests provide, by design, a variety of business-related experiences and require a great deal of thought. There are not simply right or wrong answers; instead, the tests ask you to make decisions as if you were a manager or supervisor. Because the chapters' tests are independent of one another, your score, whether high or not so high, on any one chapter's test or tests will not affect your score on any other chapter's tests. The more serious and straightforward you are as you take the tests, the more information they will give back to you, and the more accurate, meaningful, and valuable the information will be, whether you are presently a manager or supervisor, wish to become one, or are just wondering about it.

For each of the first seven attributes you will receive a managerial quotient, or mq, which is your score for that particular attribute. It will tell you the *appropriate percentile* you are in, relative to other managers and supervisors, for that attribute.

You will also receive, in the final chapter of the book, a composite MQ, which will tell you, overall, your capability as a manager. It will also tell you how you stand relative to other managers and supervisors. Said differently, it will tell you how good you are, if you're presently a manager or supervisor, or how good you would be if you were to become a manager or supervisor, or even if you are just wondering about it. Remember, MQ (in capital letters) refers to your composite Managerial Quotient, while mq (small letters) refers to any of the seven attribute managerial quotients (not including the Self-Developer).

So, there's a good deal of information to gather from the pages that follow. Take advantage of them; see how you stack up and what you can do to improve.

What You Are Going to Experience

We would like to tell you briefly what you'll be doing as you progress through the book.

In the remainder of this chapter on managerial roles we will be doing the following:

- Providing you with descriptions of the attributes.
- Giving you a short test to make sure you have a proper understanding of the attributes.
- Allowing you to see immediately how you can use the information in the book to understand how you measure up against other managers and supervisors, what your relative strengths are, and the areas that might need improvement.

- Providing you with some suggestions for getting the most out of the book.

Chapters 2 through 8 basically follow a common format. In each, you will begin with the *description of the attribute*. Then, you will be provided with *instructions and materials or information* relative to the test. At this point, *you will take the test.* As mentioned previously, the tests vary from chapter to chapter, depending on the particular attribute being measured. Finally, you will be asked to *score* your responses and calculate your *managerial quotient*, or mq, for that particular attribute.

Chapter 9, which centers on the Self-Developer, also begins with the *attribute description*. You are then asked to work out a *developmental plan for some of your attributes, based on the testing results from the previous chapters.* To come up with this developmental plan, you are provided with *almost 400 tips*, from which you will choose the most appropriate ones, given your specific circumstances.

Chapter 10 asks you to calculate your *overall MQ*, which is a *measure of your capability as a manager or supervisor.* It also provides some summary comments.

What We Are Measuring: The Attributes

Below are the eight attributes with descriptions of each. Please read these carefully, as they will be the basis for everything that follows.

The Administrator

The Administrator demonstrates behaviors associated with structuring tasks for oneself as well as for others and establishing courses of action in order to achieve specific results. Included are coordinating resources, clarifying group objectives, and establishing systems to accomplish objectives. Delegating, guiding others, following up on their activities, and establishing systems by which people are held accountable to monitor their performance against predetermined measures are also important Administrator abilities. Good Administrators manage themselves as well as others by setting up systems through which tasks can be accomplished in the most effective fashion.

The Analyzer

The Analyzer demonstrates behaviors associated with the ability to perceive and interpret information. Included are identifying critical elements or essential factors in a situation, seeing relationships, and reaching sound and logical conclusions based on available information. In addition, identifying the need for decisions, generating alternatives when necessary, and selecting strategies to implement the decisions are all part of the behavior of the Analyzer. A good Analyzer evaluates available information, sees the separate parts of the problem, draws the appropriate conclusions, and follows the necessary courses of action under the circumstances.

The Counselor

The Counselor demonstrates behaviors associated with the ability to develop effective interpersonal relationships. Included in this category are establishing rapport, listening attentively, and displaying sensitivity to others. In addition, the good Counselor is available to others when the need arises, demonstrates concern for their problems and an openness to their views and opinions, and encourages them to express their ideas and feelings. Along with these factors, a good Counselor helps others to think things through, discusses problems objectively, and presents feedback without damaging others' self-esteem.

The Communicator

The Communicator demonstrates behaviors associated with the ability to be persuasive through either written or oral communications. Included in this category are some basic presentation skills, such as using the voice effectively, choosing a vocabulary appropriate for the audience, and using effective nonverbal accompaniments such as hand gestures or eye contact to emphasize issues or points of discussion. Points should be organized so that conclusions flow logically. The good Communicator integrates the material around them and chooses the most effective words and phrases, whether to an audience of thousands or a single individual.

The Meeter

The Meeter demonstrates behaviors associated with the ability to influence others and contribute to the attainment of group goals in face-to-face situations. Included in this category are the abilities to state objectives or tasks to all concerned, to inform others of what is expected of them, to direct and coordinate others in the group, and to let others know of their importance to the success of the task at hand. Additional behaviors include helping others in the group to set and clarify goals, dealing with others in the group consistent with their needs and abilities, and holding oneself responsible for the quality and quantity of work produced. The good Meeter comes into the meeting with a prepared but not inflexible agenda, evaluates and treats other group members as individuals consistent with their own goals and needs, and attempts to participate fully and set high standards of performance for the group output. The good Meeter, no matter what his or her formal authority may be, aids the group in setting and measuring objectives consistent with their resources.

The Mentor

The Mentor demonstrates behaviors associated with developing and nurturing other individuals in order to allow them to grow to their maximum level of effectiveness in a given situation. Included in this attribute are the following abilities: evaluating other individuals' strengths and weaknesses, a willingness to work with them and offer them opportunities to try things, and providing feedback on the quality of their attempts. In addition, the good Mentor, like the good coach, gives feedback continuously, not only on results, but also on how people are accomplishing their tasks, and continuously searches for learning situations and opportunities that will allow them to grow. In other words, the Mentor develops another by establishing a close and trusting relationship, thereby establishing an environment in which the individual feels comfortable making decisions and taking risks.

The Aspirer

The Aspirer demonstrates behaviors associated with striving for a goal. The Aspirer constantly looks toward the future and works toward a greater level of perfection, a higher position, or, generally, a better position on the job or in life. The Aspirer is characterized by a great need for achievement, a willingness to work hard, and a constant focus on a goal. In addition, Aspirers gain pleasure from their achievements and, no matter the environment in which they find themselves, will continuously ask questions, search for alternative answers, and try to better their position. Aspirers will "aspire" toward perfection in managerial/supervisory situations because their values and goals are consistent with those associated with the managerial/supervisory situations.

The Self-Developer

The Self-Developer demonstrates behaviors associated with a need to develop one's own abilities to a greater degree. The Self-Developer is one who practices skills, enrolls in courses, and looks for feedback from others who are in a position to give it. In other words, the Self-Developer typically strives for a higher level of performance in key areas with which he or she is concerned. Typically, Self-Developers are comfortable working on their skills either alone or with others, are generally well organized in regard to their time and how productively they use it, and are comfortable with negative as well as positive feedback.

Do You See the Differences?

Now that we have defined the various attributes, to create a test-taking atmosphere, and to have you check your understanding of the attributes before moving along in the book, we would like you to take a very brief test. Turn to the next page, *The Attribute Understanding Test;* read the instructions, then complete the test. When you have finished, turn to the *Answer Key,* and follow those instructions as well.

ATTRIBUTE UNDERSTANDING TEST

This test measures your understanding of the eight basic attributes. On the left-hand side of this page are the attributes, numbered 1 through 8. On the right-hand side of the page is a list of 16 brief statements, lettered a through p. On the line next to each statement, write the number of the attribute that corresponds to it (only one attribute per statement). You may use a separate sheet of paper in responding to this if you like. Each attribute is to be used twice.

Attribute

1. Administrator
2. Analyzer
3. Counselor
4. Communicator
5. Meeter
6. Mentor
7. Aspirer
8. Self-Developer

Statements

____ a. Has a strong desire for achievement in management situations

____ b. Uses good voice inflection when speaking

____ c. Aids in setting group objectives

____ d. Is able to delegate

____ e. Interprets information

____ f. Displays sensitivity to others

____ g. Nurtures other individuals

____ h. Works on developing own attributes

____ i. Looks for feedback on own performance

____ j. Offers others opportunities to try things

____ k. Establishes systems

____ l. Sees relationships between various pieces of information

____ m. Develops effective interpersonal relationships

____ n. Uses good choice of words to deliver a message

____ o. Searches to identify new learning experiences for others

____ p. Strives for a goal

Answer Key

Below are the correct answers to the *Attribute Understanding Test.* Please check your answers against them, and write the total number correct in the space below.

a. __7__	e. __2__	i. __8__	m. __3__
b. __4__	f. __3__	j. __5__	n. __4__
c. __5__	g. __6__	k. __1__	o. __6__
d. __1__	h. __8__	l. __2__	p. __7__

Write the number correct here _____.

If your score was at least __14__, move along in the book.

If your score was __13 or less__, review the descriptions again (pages 4–8) before moving along in the book.

A Glimpse of How You Can Use the Results from the Tests

As we said before, the combination of competency factors and attitudinal factors a person possesses determines to a large extent whether or not he or she is likely to be successful as a manager or a supervisor. Without the proper competency factors, mastery of management/supervisory responsibilities is difficult to achieve. Likewise, without the proper attitudinal factors, mastery of managerial/supervisory responsibilities would also be difficult. Competency factors and attitudinal factors can best be thought of as two pieces of a "performance puzzle." Without a proper relationship between the two, the puzzle cannot be solved. Figure 1.1 illustrates this relationship.

We all have different combinations of attributes, and we all differ to some extent in terms of the degree to which we display them. This leads to some very different ways of operating, as well as different likelihoods of success. The ideal manager/supervisor excels on all the competency factors and is exemplary with respect to the attitudinal factors. Unfortunately, there are very few people we can say this about. As you work through the book, each chapter will give you an oppor-

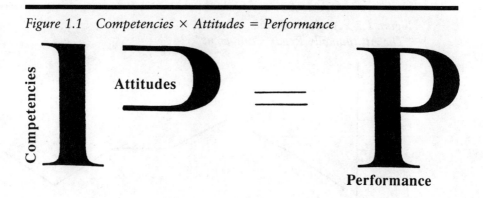

Figure 1.1   Competencies × Attitudes = Performance

tunity to evaluate your own level in each competency and attitudinal factor. When you have completed the book, you will be able to put those evaluations, your mq's, together to form an attribute profile of your own relative strengths and weaknesses as well as an overall MQ.

Comparing yourself to others will make your own test results clearer and more meaningful. Therefore, in Figures 1.2 through 1.7 we graphically illustrate some of the more typical patterns we have found. Any one or more of these attribute profiles may apply to you; the possibilities are pretty much unlimited. Each attribute profile has a descriptive label and a brief interpretation. Please review these now and refer to them as you progress through the book. As you work through the chapters, and score your own attributes, you will want to concentrate your developmental efforts on those that are not, relative to these attribute profiles, as high as you would like.

Suggestions for Progressing Through the Book

Here are some suggestions for you as you work through the remaining chapters. Keeping these in mind will help you to get as much as you possibly can out of the book.

Figure 1.2   Attribute Profile
"The Attitudinally Ready Competent"

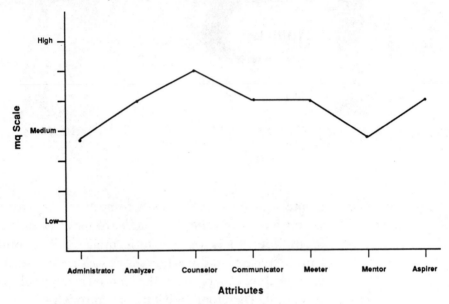

Interpretation:
1. Overall competent, and attitude is acceptable
2. Could use some development, but not deficient

1. As is true in many areas of life, what you put into something is precisely what you'll get out of it. So, put as much effort into working through this book as you can.
2. Answer the test questions honestly, in ways that will reflect the real you; don't respond according to how you think we might want you to respond, or how other people might respond. This would not be an accurate gauge of who you truly are.
3. Related to the above suggestion, particularly with regard to the attitudinal factor tests in Chapters 7 and 8, answer in a straightforward way; do not try to outguess the test. It won't give you a true reflection of yourself.

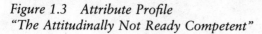

Figure 1.3   Attribute Profile
"The Attitudinally Not Ready Competent"

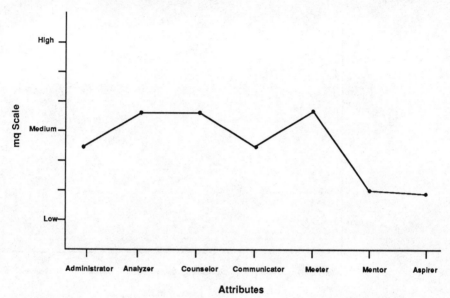

Interpretation:
1. No real deficiencies in competencies
2. Attitude to be (or continue to be) a manager/supervisor is low

4. The book is intended to make you think, as well as act. Make sure to do both.
5. In working through the tests in Chapters 2 through 8, you may either write in the book or use a legal-size pad, following the format of the tests.
6. As you respond to test items, you may refer to any pertinent material contained in the given chapter.
7. It will be helpful if you read and do the tests in each chapter during one continuous period of time.

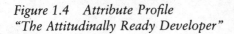

Figure 1.4   Attribute Profile
"The Attitudinally Ready Developer"

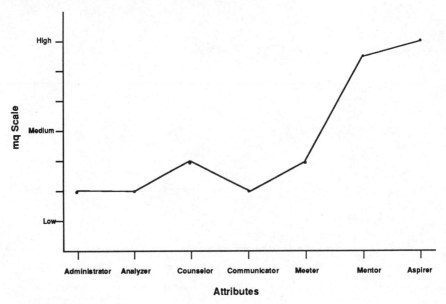

Interpretation:
1. Attitude to do (or continue to do) managerial/supervisory activities is high
2. But very much in need of competency development

8. Again, most of all, put as much as you can into this book, so you will get as much as you possibly can out of it.

Now, having read these suggestions, you are ready to begin.

Figure 1.5   *Attribute Profile*
"The Attitudinally Not Ready Developer"

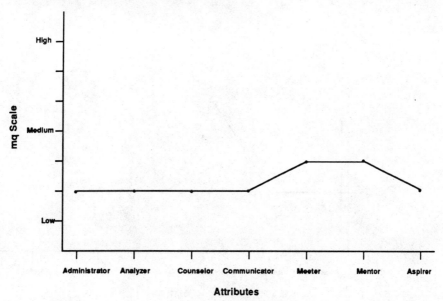

Interpretation:
1. Very much in need of competency development
2. Attitude to be (or continue to be) a manager/supervisor is low
3. Should seek opportunities other than managerial/supervisory activities

Figure 1.6   Attribute Profile
"The People Competent"

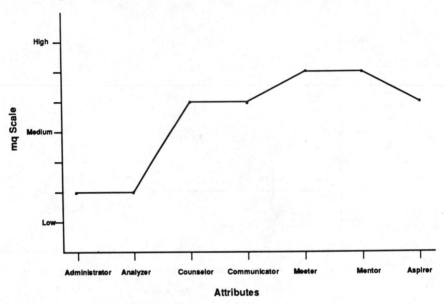

Interpretation:
1. High on people competencies; low on data competencies
2. Attitude is acceptable
3. Needs to work on data competencies (nonpeople competencies)

Figure 1.7   Attribute Profile
"The Data Competent"

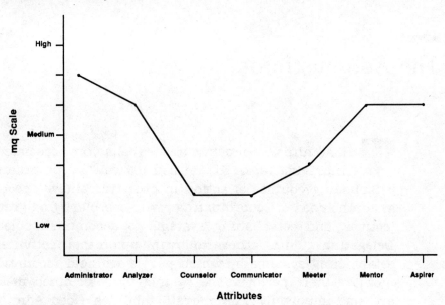

Interpretation:
1. High on data competencies; low on people competencies
2. Attitude is acceptable
3. Needs to work on people competencies (nondata competencies)

CHAPTER 2

The Administrator

THE Administrator demonstrates behaviors associated with structuring tasks for oneself as well as for others and establishing courses of action in order to achieve specific results. Included are coordinating resources, clarifying group objectives, and establishing systems to accomplish objectives. Delegating, guiding others, following up on their activities, and establishing systems by which people are held accountable to monitor their performance against predetermined measures are also important Administrator abilities. Good Administrators manage themselves as well as others by setting up systems through which tasks can be accomplished in the most effective fashion.

In this chapter, you will find a test designed to help you assess your own Administrator attribute.

Instructions and Test Materials

For the purpose of this exercise, you are to consider yourself Chris Miller, the newly appointed Production Manager for Fashionable Fashions, Inc. This Tennessee-based company manufactures a full clothing line for adolescents. As Production Manager within the Formal Wear Division, you are responsible for all phases of clothing production, from receipt of materials through distribution of finished garments.

Today is Friday, March 24, 10:00 A.M., and you have just returned early from your vacation due to the unexpected resignation of your supervisor, Bea Williams, Director of Plant Operations. Top management has asked you to assume her responsibilities in addition to your own until a replacement can be found.

Your task in this exercise is to read through the materials on the following pages and then answer questions related to these materials. The materials consist of 20 administrative items that might be handled by either a production manager or an operations manager. Because the items often relate to each other, you will need to study them carefully. The 25 multiple-choice questions that follow address the various issues mentioned in the items.

Figure 2.1: Fashionable Fashions, Inc. Organizational Chart

	VICE PRESIDENT FORMAL WEAR DIVISION John Weibe	
DIRECTOR OF FINANCE Louis Morrison	DIRECTOR OF PLANT OPERATIONS Bea Williams ADMINISTRATIVE ASSISTANT Lori Myers	DIRECTOR OF SALES AND MARKETING Michael Weller
MAINTENANCE MANAGER Ted Glasson	PRODUCTION MANAGER Chris Miller	WAREHOUSE MANAGER Terry Jones
SHIPPING AND RECEIVING SUPERVISOR Diane Jarvis	FIRST SHIFT SUPERVISOR Brian Manley	SECOND SHIFT SUPERVISOR Nancy Bradley
	PRODUCTION EMPLOYEES	PRODUCTION EMPLOYEES

Item 2.1

Fashionable Fashions, Inc.
Memorandum

TO: Chris Miller, Production Manager
FROM: John Weibe, Vice President, Formal Wear Division
DATE: March 22
RE: Temporary Assignment

First, let me say how much I appreciate your assuming Bea Williams's duties. I realize these extra responsibilities will present quite a challenge for you. Please let me know if there is anything I can do to help.

There is one thing that needs your immediate attention. For the third week in a row, the time cards from the second shift have been incorrectly filled out. Louis Morrison, Director of Finance, is concerned that these will present problems in the upcoming corporate audit. Please look into this right away.

Item 2.2   Weekly Production Report

March

Shift 1

Week	Pieces Produced	Total MTD*	Total YTD*	Last Year TD*	% Change	Weekly Plan	% to Plan**
1	60,000	60,000	220,000	250,000	−12	62,500	−4
2	52,220	112,000	272,220	300,000	−9	60,000	−13
3	51,000	163,220	323,220	345,000	−6	60,000	−15
4	—	—	—	—	—	—	—

Shift 2

Week	Pieces Produced	Total MTD*	Total YTD*	Last Year TD*	% Change	Weekly Plan	% to Plan**
1	40,000	40,000	180,000	250,000	−28	62,500	−36
2	37,800	77,800	217,800	290,000	−25	60,000	−37
3	34,000	111,800	251,800	350,000	−28	60,000	−43
4	—	—	—	—	—	—	—

*MTD = Month to date; YTD = year to date; TD = to date
**% to plan = How close results are to the plan; for example, for week 1, weekly plan was 62,500; pieces produced for week were 60,000; 62,500 minus 60,000 = 2,500; 2,500/60,000 = −4%

Item 2.3

Fashionable Fashions, Inc.
Memorandum

TO: Bea Williams, Director of Plant Operations
FROM: Michael Weller, Director of Sales and Marketing
DATE: March 23
RE: Late Shipments

For some reason, I am receiving complaints from our customers that their shipments have been arriving late. I don't have to tell you the problems this causes for us. I would appreciate you looking into this matter, so we may straighten out this problem as soon as possible.

Item 2.4

Fashionable Fashions, Inc.
Memorandum

TO: Bea Williams, Director of Plant Operations
FROM: Lori Myers, Administrative Assistant
DATE: March 22
RE: Phone Message

Bea,
While you were out Diane Jarvis called and just wanted to let you know that they still don't have enough work to keep them busy. So most of the time they are just sitting around in the afternoons.

Item 2.5

Payroll Budget
March

	Maintenance		Production		Warehouse	
Week	Budgeted Hours	Actual Hours	Budgeted Hours	Actual Hours	Budgeted Hours	Actual Hours
1	200	160	1200	1500	200	210
2	200	120	1200	1350	200	190
3	200	115	1200	1300	200	210
4	—	—	—	—	—	—

Item 2.6

Fashionable Fashions, Inc.
Memorandum

TO: Bea Williams, Director of Plant Operations
FROM: Terry Jones, Warehouse Manager
DATE: March 21
RE: Leaky Roof

I felt that it was time to let you know that we've got a leaky roof in the south end of the warehouse. I've contacted Ted Glasson, Maintenance Manager, several times about this but have gotten no response. It's getting so bad now that merchandise has been damaged. I really need your help on this matter.

Item 2.7

Fashionable Fashions, Inc.
Memorandum

TO: All Divisional Vice Presidents
FROM: Corporate Planning
DATE: March 23
RE: Seasonal Forecast—Spring and Summer

We are glad to report that we now expect an unplanned 20 percent increase over last year in customer orders in the upcoming season. This is due to the excellent job by our Sales and Marketing Department and to Operations for turning out such high-quality merchandise. Let's keep our customers satisfied by continuing to produce high-quality products.

Bea,
The forecast is great
but it means more
work for us. I know
we can handle it!

John

Item 2.8

Fashionable Fashions, Inc.
Memorandum

TO: Bea Williams, Director of Plant Operations
FROM: Invoice Office
DATE: March 21
RE: Inventory Discrepancy

This memo pertains to a shipment of buttons from the Acme Button Company on March 1. The paperwork from the warehouse shows that they received 1000 units. Acme is billing us for 2000 units. We have spoken to Terry Jones, the Warehouse Manager, about this matter several times, but Terry seems unable to solve this problem. Please see what you can do.

Item 2.9

Fashionable Fashions, Inc.
Memorandum

TO: John Weibe, Vice President—Formal Wear Division
FROM: Jan Caroll, Vice President—Sportswear Division
DATE: March 20
RE: Request for Warehouse Volunteers

I hope you can help me out with a problem I am having. Three of my warehouse staff have retired or been transferred in the past few weeks. Up until now, we've been able to handle the work load, but we are beginning to fall behind. Maybe some of your part-time warehouse personnel could use some extra hours. Could you please ask for volunteers? We could use as many as four. Thanks for your help in this matter.

Chris,
Please handle and
let Jan know what,
if anything, we can
do.   John

Item 2.10

Fashionable Fashions, Inc.
Memorandum

TO: Bea Williams, Director of Plant Operations
FROM: Corporate Personnel
DATE: March 20
RE: Community Relations Seminar

This is to inform you that we scheduled a Community Relations Seminar for Monday, April 12, at 10:00 A.M. We would like to see all divisional directors attend. Please contact Joan Mason at ext. 370 by April 1 to let her know if you can attend.

Item 2.11

Fashionable Fashions, Inc.
Memorandum

TO: Bea Williams, Director of Plant Operations
FROM: Training Department
DATE: March 21
RE: New Equipment Training Course

As you know, we are about to computerize our inventory system in the warehouse. The following people need to be trained on this new system. Please make sure they can attend one of the following training sessions:

April 1   10:00 A.M.
April 1   2:00 P.M.
April 3   10:00 A.M.

Warehouse personnel: Susan Atkins
                       Linda Forbes
                       Steve Gains

If there is a problem with these times, please contact us.

Item 2.12

Fashionable Fashions, Inc.
Memorandum

TO: Chris Miller, Production Manager
FROM: Personnel
DATE: March 19
RE: Accident Report on Dan Riley, First Shift Worker

On March 12, Dan Riley reported an accident to Personnel. We still have not received an accident report from your department. Please forward this as soon as possible.

Item 2.13

Fashionable Fashions, Inc.
Memorandum

TO: Chris Miller, Production Manager
FROM: Lori Myers, Administrative Assistant
DATE: March 24
RE: Phone Message

Chris,
While you were out John Weibe called to inform you that attendance at the April 12th all-day staff meeting is mandatory. You will need to present your seasonal report at this time.

Item 2.14

Fashionable Fashions, Inc.
Memorandum

TO: Chris Miller, Production Manager
FROM: Nancy Bradley, Second Shift Supervisor
DATE: March 19
RE: Procedure Change

I have been observing one of our production lines and feel that production can be increased by rearranging some of our equipment. As it is now, the cutters have to walk all the way around the supply table to deposit their finished work. Not only is this time-consuming, but it is a safety hazard, especially during peak hours. I would like your permission to rearrange the work area.

Item 2.15

Fashionable Fashions, Inc.
Memorandum

TO: Bea Williams, Director of Plant Operations
FROM: Randy Sommers, Personnel Director
DATE: March 23
RE: Profit Sharing Meetings

Our annual Profit Sharing Meetings will begin on April 6th and continue through April 9th. All meetings will be held at 10:00 A.M. in the employee lounge and will last approximately two hours. The next set of meetings will be held in May, so employees who are unable to attend in April can be scheduled later.

Bea,
   Just wanted to let you know that we haven't received the United Way pledge cards back from your Maintenance Department. Could you please take care of this?

      Randy

Item 2.16

Frank Russell
Creative Consulting, Inc.
123 143rd St.
New York, NY 10012

March 20

Dear Manager:

In this day and age, the marketplace has become a highly competitive place. The key to a company's success is how well it can sell and market its products. Of course, a company is only as good as its managers—this is especially true in sales and marketing departments. Such positions require public contact and put added pressure on these managers.

Using a host of well developed and tested techniques, Creative Consulting can help your company get the best out of sales and marketing managers. In business for over 10 years, Creative Consulting has successfully served over 300 private and public organizations. We think the seminars we offer can improve your sales and marketing techniques and benefit your whole organization.

I am enclosing a brochure which details the kind of seminars we offer as well as the upcoming seminar schedule. If you or anyone in your organization is interested in attending these seminars, call Larry Miller at (212) 555-1234. We hope to see you there.

Sincerely,

Frank Russell

Frank Russell

Enclosure
FR/ccr

Item 2.17

Fashionable Fashions, Inc.
Memorandum

TO: Terry Jones, Warehouse Manager
FROM: Central Purchasing
DATE: March 19
RE: Large Shipment

Wanted to let you know that the ABC Fabric shipment you ordered will arrive at your warehouse on April 1. It's a very large shipment—30,000 cartons—which will require extensive space. You may need to start making accommodations for this shipment right away.

Bea,
    I'm not sure we
can handle a
Shipment this large.
            Terry

Item 2.18

March 24

Dear Chris,

First let me say I'm looking forward to working with you in your new capacity. I'll be glad to help you in any way I can.

I hate to start off by giving you a problem, but there is one thing I would like to mention right away. Production figures from department managers for the weekly report are consistently getting to me late. Part of the problem is that I'm having to deal with four different clericals, so any problems require that I track the person down first. This can be very time-consuming. On top of that, the departments don't have the same person prepare the figures each week. So far, I have managed to get the weekly reports done on time, but it has really been a strain.

Lori

Item 2.19

Fashionable Fashions, Inc.
Memorandum

TO: Bea Williams, Director of Plant Operations
FROM: Lori Myers, Administrative Assistant
DATE: March 24
RE: Phone Message

Bea,
While you were out Michael Weller, the Director of Sales and Marketing, called. He has a priority shipment in production that must be out by Monday. Brian told him that it was too late to get it out—he didn't realize it was a priority shipment.

Item 2.20

Fashionable Fashions, Inc.
Memorandum

TO: All Directors
FROM: John Weibe, Vice President, Formal Wear Division
DATE: March 18
RE: Promotable Employees

As you know, it is a policy of Fashionable Fashions, Inc. to promote from within the organization whenever possible. To achieve this, we need to identify promotable employees so that proper guidance and training can be provided. Please forward a list of promotable employees in your area. There is no rush on this—Corporate Personnel doesn't need any names until July 1.

THE ADMINISTRATOR TEST

We would now like you to answer the 25 multiple-choice questions that pertain to the 20 items you have just reviewed. For each question, based on the information provided in the items, choose the one statement that best answers the question. It may be the action you should take *first,* not the only action you should take (e.g., see questions 1 and 2). You may refer back to the items as you do the test.

_____1. With respect to Item 2.1, the memorandum from John Weibe, Vice President, concerning the time card problem, and any possible related items, which of the following actions *should* you take?
   a. Call Louis Morrison, Director of Finance, and ask him to get in touch with Nancy Bradley, Second Shift Supervisor, to correct the problem.
   b. Call Nancy Bradley, Second Shift Supervisor, and instruct her to find out the problem employees' names and report these to you.
   c. Call Nancy Bradley, Second Shift Supervisor, and instruct her to handle the problem.
   d. Call Louis Morrison, Director of Finance, for a list of problem employees, and then discuss the problem with each of these employees.

_____2. With respect to Item 2.1, the memorandum from John Weibe, Vice President, concerning the time card problem, and any possible related items, which of the following follow-up actions *should* you take?
   a. Call Nancy Bradley, Second Shift Supervisor, to find out if the problem has been solved.
   b. Make a note to check the time cards before the end of the next pay period to see whether the problem has been solved.
   c. Call Louis Morrison, Director of Finance, to ask him to follow up.
   d. Wait to see if any more complaints come in from Louis Morrison, Director of Finance.

_____3. With respect to Item 2.2, the Weekly Production Report for March, and any possible related items, which of the following actions *should* you take?
   a. Meet with Nancy Bradley, Second Shift Supervisor, to discuss the production figures.
   b. Meet individually with Brian Manley and Nancy Bradley, Shift Supervisors, to discuss the production figures.
   c. Have one meeting with both Brian Manley and Nancy Bradley, Shift Supervisors, to discuss the production figures.
   d. Postpone action until fourth-week figures are in.

———4. With respect to Item 2.2, the Weekly Production Report for March, and any possible related items, which of the following actions *should* you take to resolve the production problem?
   a. Have Shift Supervisors meet with their employees for a pep talk to increase productivity.
   b. Have Shift Supervisors compile production records on each employee to identify individual problems.
   c. Tell Shift Supervisors that declines in production will not be tolerated any longer.
   d. Require Shift Supervisors to submit production figures to you on a daily basis.

———5. With respect to Item 2.3, the memorandum from Michael Weller, Director of Sales and Marketing, concerning the late shipments, and any possible related items, which of the following actions *should* you take?
   a. Tell Michael Weller, Director of Sales and Marketing, that you cannot handle this problem right now, given other things you need to do.
   b. Call Diane Jarvis, Shipping and Receiving Supervisor, and tell her to start getting shipments out on time.
   c. Authorize overtime in production to get the products out on time.
   d. Reassign shipping and receiving staff to production on at least a temporary basis to increase production output.

———6. With respect to Item 2.4, the phone message from Diane Jarvis, Shipping and Receiving Supervisor, concerning spare time in the Shipping and Receiving Department, and any possible related items, which of the following actions *should* you take?
   a. Tell Diane Jarvis, Shipping and Receiving Supervisor, to lay off extra staff (on a seniority basis).
   b. Have Diane Jarvis, Shipping and Receiving Supervisor, reassign her extra staff to the Warehouse, Maintenance, and Production Departments.

c. Have Diane Jarvis, Shipping and Receiving Supervisor, send people over to the Production Department as soon as they run out of daily work.

d. Have Diane Jarvis, Shipping and Receiving Supervisor, meet with Shift Supervisors to reschedule her extra staff into Production Departments.

_____7. With respect to Item 2.5, the Payroll Budget Report for March, and any possible related items, which of the following actions *should* you take?

a. No immediate response is necessary.

b. Call the Shift Supervisors to find out why their actual hours are more than their budgeted hours.

c. Call Ted Glasson, Maintenance Manager, to find out why their actual hours are less than their planned hours.

d. Call both the Shift Supervisors and the Maintenance Manager to find out why there is a discrepancy between their planned and actual hours.

_____8. With respect to Item 2.6, the memorandum from Terry Jones, Warehouse Manager, concerning the leaky roof, and any possible related items, which of the following actions *should* you take?

a. Tell Terry Jones, Warehouse Manager, that you are sure Maintenance will get to it when they can.

b. Meet with Ted Glasson, Maintenance Manager, as soon as possible to determine why there has been no response, and the reason for the leaky roof.

c. Tell Ted Glasson, Maintenance Manager, to fix the leaky roof immediately.

d. Ask Terry Jones, Warehouse Manager, to meet with Ted Glasson, Maintenance Manager, to solve the problem on their own.

_____9. With respect to Item 2.6, the memorandum from Terry Jones, Warehouse Manager, concerning the leaky roof, and any possible related items, which of the following actions *should* you take, to prevent this problem from happening again? In responding to this question, assume that the problem with getting the leaky roof fixed was due to poor prioritizing of work load by Ted Glasson, Maintenance Manager.

a. Find out how Ted Glasson, Maintenance Manager, has been prioritizing the work load, and help revise this system if necessary.

b. Tell Ted Glasson, Maintenance Manager, to begin doing a better job at prioritizing the work load.

c. Instruct Ted Glasson, Maintenance Manager, to check with you on a daily basis so that you can prioritize the work load.

d. Continue to check with Ted Glasson, Maintenance Manager, regularly to help him prioritize the work load.

———10. With respect to Item 2.7, the memorandum from Corporate Planning, concerning the seasonal forecast, and any possible related items, which of the following actions *should* you take?

a. Write a memorandum to notify the management staff regarding the increase in orders now expected.

b. Have each manager describe the impact this increase will have on his department so that appropriate steps can be taken.

c. Review the budgets from each department yourself, and make the appropriate plans to handle the increase.

d. Call personnel and tell them to hire extra workers to start in March.

———11. With respect to Item 2.8, the memorandum from the Invoice Office, concerning the inventory discrepancy, and any possible related items, which of the following actions *should* you take?

a. Work with Terry Jones, Warehouse Manager, as soon as possible, for the purpose of correcting the problem.

b. Forward the memorandum to Terry Jones, Warehouse Manager, with instructions to correct the problem.

c. Delegate the problem to Lori Myers, Administrative Assistant.

d. Postpone action on this problem until you have more time.

———12. With respect to Item 2.9, the memorandum from Jan Caroll, Vice President of the Sportswear Division, concerning the request for warehouse volunteers, and any possible related items, which of the following actions *should* you take?

a. Post a notice in the employee lounge requesting the volunteers.

b. Ask Terry Jones, Warehouse Manager, to handle the situation.

c. Pick the volunteers yourself.

d. Advise Jan Caroll, Vice President of the Sportswear Division, that no volunteers are available at this time.

___13. With respect to Item 2.10, the memorandum from Corporate Personnel concerning the Community Relations Seminar, and any possible related items, which of the following actions *should* you take?

a. Advise Joan Mason of Personnel that you will attend the seminar on April 12.

b. Advise Joan Mason of Personnel that you will be unable to attend the seminar on April 12.

c. Have Lori Myers, Administrative Assistant, attend the seminar in your place.

d. Request that Corporate Personnel reschedule the seminar for 2:00 P.M.

___14. With respect to Item 2.11, the memorandum from the Training Department, concerning the new equipment training course, and any possible related items, which of the following actions *should* you take?

a. Notify Terry Jones, Warehouse Manager, that the employees mentioned in the memo should be scheduled.

b. Personally contact and schedule each employee to attend the course.

c. Meet with the three employees as a group and tell them you would like them to attend.

d. Give each worker mentioned in the memorandum a copy of the memorandum.

___15. With respect to Item 2.12, the memorandum from Personnel, concerning the accident report on Dan Riley, and any possible related items, which of the following actions *should* you take?

a. Have the employee complete the accident report form and forward it to Personnel himself.
b. Postpone action until you have more time to take care of it.
c. Have Lori Myers, Administrative Assistant, fill out the accident report form and forward it to Personnel.
d. Forward the memorandum to Brian Manley, First Shift Supervisor, with a note to take immediate action.

_____16. With respect to Item 2.14, the memorandum from Nancy Bradley, Second Shift Supervisor, concerning a procedure change, and any possible related items, which of the following actions *should* you take?
a. Ask Nancy Bradley, Second Shift Supervisor, to submit a formal request to John Weibe, Vice President.
b. Inform Nancy Bradley, Second Shift Supervisor, that the request cannot be accepted at this time.
c. Plan to meet with Nancy Bradley and Brian Manley, Shift Supervisors, to discuss the request.
d. Instruct Nancy Bradley, Second Shift Supervisor, to rearrange the equipment as she sees fit.

_____17. With respect to Item 2.15, the memorandum from Randy Sommers, Personnel Director, concerning the profit sharing meetings, and any possible related items, which of the following actions *should* you take?
a. Post a memorandum in the employee lounge announcing the profit sharing meetings.
b. Plan to schedule employees to attend the May meetings, due to current work loads.
c. Send copies of the memorandum to each manager and supervisor asking them to determine for their group of subordinates whether the April or May meetings would be more appropriate, given work demands.
d. Send a memorandum to Personnel stating that the April and May meetings present difficulties, and you would prefer rescheduling the meetings in June.

___18. With respect to Item 2.15, the memorandum from Randy Sommers, Personnel Director, concerning the United Way pledge cards, and any possible related items, which of the following actions *should* you take?
   a. Make a note to call Ted Glasson, Maintenance Manager, and tell him to get the United Way pledge cards returned to Randy Sommers.
   b. Forward the memorandum to Ted Glasson, Maintenance Manager, with a note to please take care of the United Way pledge cards and get back to Randy Sommers regarding them.
   c. Postpone action on the United Way pledge card problem until you have more time.
   d. Go to the Maintenance Department yourself to collect the United Way pledge cards.

___19. With respect to Item 2.16, the letter from Frank Russell at Creative Consulting, concerning the sales and marketing seminars, and any possible related items, which of the following actions *should* you take?
   a. Throw the letter away.
   b. Forward the letter to Michael Weller, Director of Sales and Marketing.
   c. Forward the letter to the management staff.
   d. Forward the letter to John Weibe, Vice President.

___20. With respect to Item 2.16, the letter from Frank Russell at Creative Consulting, concerning the sales and marketing seminars, and any possible related items, which of the following actions *should* you take, with regard to future mail?
   a. Have Lori Myers, Administrative Assistant, write to Creative Consulting asking them to remove you from their mailing list.
   b. In the future, have Lori Myers, Administrative Assistant, screen the mail, using a set of guidelines that the two of you develop.
   c. In the future, have Lori Myers, Administrative Assistant, screen the mail and not forward any irrelevant mail to you.
   d. Have the mail room not forward any correspondence that is not specifically addressed to you.

___21. With respect to Item 2.17, the memorandum from Central Purchasing, concerning the large shipment, and any possible related items, which of the following actions *should* you take?

a. Postpone action on this matter until you have more time.

b. Send a note to Terry Jones, Warehouse Manager, telling him to solve the problem in any way he sees fit.

c. Call Terry and have him immediately call Central Purchasing to tell them it can be done.

d. Call Terry and have him immediately call Central Purchasing in order to get together with them to see what the possible solutions are.

___22. With respect to Item 2.18, the letter from Lori Myers, Administrative Assistant, concerning late production figures from the departments, and any possible related items, which of the following actions *should* you take?

a. Plan to call a meeting Monday with managers to discuss the problem.

b. Send a memorandum to the managers stating that they must get the figures in on time.

c. Instruct all managers to arrange for one clerical to collect all figures on a permanent basis.

d. Postpone any action on this matter until you are able to speak with Lori to make sure there are no other issues associated with it.

___23. With respect to Item 2.19, the phone message from Michael Weller, Director of Sales and Marketing, concerning the late shipment, and any possible related items, which of the following actions *should* you take?

a. Call Brian Manley, First Shift Supervisor, and tell him to get the shipment out immediately.

b. Help Brian Manley, First Shift Supervisor, reorganize his work load in order to get the shipment out immediately.

c. Call Michael Weller, Director of Sales and Marketing, and apologize for not getting the shipment out.

d. Call Brian Manley, First Shift Supervisor, to find out why the shipment is late getting out.

_____24. With respect to Item 2.19, the phone message from Michael Weller, Director of Sales and Marketing, concerning the late shipment, and any possible related items, which of the following actions *should* you take, to ensure that the same problem does not happen again?

a. Arrange with Michael Weller, Director of Sales and Marketing, to get a list of priority shipments sent to the Production Department weekly.

b. Call Michael Weller, Director of Sales and Marketing, and ask him not to wait until it is too late to inform you of a problem next time.

c. Arrange for Shift Supervisors to call Michael Weller, Director of Sales and Marketing, weekly for a list of priority shipments.

d. Send a memorandum to John Weibe, Vice President, saying that better coordination of priority shipments is required.

_____25. With respect to Item 2.20, the memorandum from John Weibe, Vice President, concerning promotable employees, and any possible related items, which of the following actions *should* you take?

a. Compile a list of employees and send it back to John Weibe, Vice President.

b. Request, from Personnel, a copy of performance reviews for all your employees.

c. Send a memorandum at your earliest convenience to all managers and supervisors requesting a list of their promotable employees.

d. Instruct Lori Myers, Administrative Assistant, to write a memorandum to managers and supervisors requesting a list of their promotable employees.

Scoring the Administrator Test

On the following pages are the correct answers to the multiple-choice questions. Accompanying each correct answer is a short explanation.

1. Compare your choice to the correct answer on all 25 questions. Place a check mark by each question you answered correctly. Be sure to read the explanation for the correct choice for each question.
2. Add up the check marks. The sum can range from 0 to 25.
3. Write the sum in the space below.

My score on the Administrator Test is _____ .

Correct Answers and Explanations

Q#	ANS	Explanation
1.	a.	This problem lends itself to delegation because it is simple enough to be handled by Nancy Bradley, Second Shift Supervisor. Your time is too valuable to spend on such a matter.
2.	b.	This is the easiest and most expedient way to *ensure* that the problem has been solved.
3.	c.	Because both shifts are having production problems, the most efficient way to gather information about the problem is to meet with both Shift Supervisors. This is especially true since a solution to the problem may require coordination between the two shifts.
4.	b.	By monitoring individual performance, you and the Supervisors can identify and take concrete action toward solving the production problem.
5.	d.	Because Diane Jarvis, Shipping and Receiving Supervisor, informed you that her staff was not busy (Item 2.4), this is the most efficient and cost effective means to solve this problem.
6.	d.	Since production needs the extra help, the most effective reassignment of staff would be to production areas. Having Diane Jarvis, Shipping and Receiving Supervisor, meet with the Production Supervisors will ensure that reassignment is organized and well coordinated.
7.	d.	You need to gather information from the two other managers because all three departments are showing discrepancies. This information will aid you in future planning.

____ 8.   b.   There could be something else underlying this problem; for example, excessive work load for the Maintenance Department; or a bad relationship between Ted and Terry. Meeting with Ted should provide the proper understanding of the situation. Also, this action will most likely get the problem solved, that is, repairing the leaky roof.

____ 9.   a.   The best way to ensure that future work gets done effectively is to help organize a system to provide guidelines on a continuing basis. This also allows Ted Glasson, Maintenance Manager, to function more independently, freeing up more of your time.

____10.   b.   This problem requires planning to handle the extra work load. In order to devise the best plan, you need to gather information from all departments affected by the forecast.

____11.   a.   Working with Terry Jones, Warehouse Manager, will ensure that the problem will be solved in a timely fashion. Also, it will provide a learning experience for Terry so that he can solve similar problems in the future.

____12.   b.   This problem lends itself to delegation because it is simple enough to be handled by Terry Jones, Warehouse Manager. Also, Terry is in the best position to judge whether personnel are available to volunteer for other work.

____13.   b.   You will be unable to attend the seminar due to a conflict with the mandatory staff meeting called by John Weibe, Vice President (Item 2.13).

____14.   a.   This problem lends itself to delegation because it is simple enough to be handled by Terry Jones, Warehouse Manager. Also, Terry is in the best position to schedule the employees mentioned.

____15. d. This problem is simple enough to delegate, and Brian Manley, First Shift Supervisor, is clearly responsible for his workers.

____16. c. Since effective planning in an organization requires information from all those affected by the plan, it should be discussed with both Shift Supervisors.

____17. c. While current work loads may be high for some departments, it is best to leave the decisions regarding April or May to the people in the best position to know, the immediate supervisor or manager. Delaying it to June ignores the needs of the employees.

____18. b. In terms of your own time, this is the most expedient way to handle the problem. The nature of the problem is such that it does not require immediate action such as phone contact with Ted Glasson.

____19. b. Since the letter pertains to Sales and Marketing, it should be forwarded to Michael Weller, Director of Sales and Marketing.

____20. b. This will help ensure that you save time in the future by not receiving any irrelevant mail. It also will structure the task for Lori Myers, Administrative Assistant, by defining "irrelevant" mail.

____21. d. Coordinating resources in this kind of situation will lead to the most effective solution to the problem. Also, immediate attention is required.

____22. d. There isn't a real urgency associated with this problem, and speaking to Lori first will allow you to see if there are any other issues involved, including perhaps possible problems with Lori.

____23. b. You can best ensure that the priority shipment is completed by restructuring the production work load with Brian Manley, First Shift Supervisor.

_____24. a. This action results in the most direct and efficient long-term solution to the problem.

_____25. c. This choice recognizes that immediate attention is not required *and* that it is a sensitive enough issue for you to ask for the information directly from your managers and supervisors.

Calculating and Interpreting Your Administrator mq

1. Write your score again here _____ .

2. Calculate your mq by dividing your score by 25, and then multiplying by 100. Place your answer directly below.*

$$\frac{\text{My total score}}{25} \times 100 = \text{_____ Administrator mq.}$$

* Round off the result to the nearest whole number. Your mq can range from 0 to 100.

Interpretation of mq

An mq of at least 75 indicates satisfactory performance with respect to the attribute being measured. It essentially means that you earned at least 75 percent of the total possible score. This 75 percent level associated with satisfactory performance is based upon our collective experience with thousands of people taking managerial/supervisory attribute tests. As your mq approaches 100, it becomes more and more exceptional. If your mq is in the 90's, you would find yourself in approximately the top 10 percent of the test takers. With an mq in the 80's, this would place you in the top 30 percent of test takers, and an mq of 75 would mean you were in the top 50 percent of test takers. An mq of below 75 would put you in the bottom 50 percent of test takers.

Developmentally speaking, any mq of below 75 would indicate an attribute in need of development. This will be discussed in further detail in Chapter 9.

CHAPTER 3

The Analyzer

The Analyzer demonstrates behaviors associated with the ability to perceive and interpret information. Included are identifying critical elements or essential factors in a situation, seeing relationships, and reaching sound and logical conclusions based on available information. In addition, identifying the need for decisions, generating alternatives when necessary, and selecting strategies to implement the decisions are all part of the behavior of the Analyzer. A good Analyzer evaluates available information, sees the separate parts of the problem, draws the appropriate conclusions, and follows the necessary courses of action under the circumstances.

In this chapter you will find a test designed to help you assess your own Analyzer attribute.

Instructions and Test Materials

For the purpose of this exercise, you are to consider yourself Gerry Clark, General Manager of Paradise Isle, a new luxury resort complex opening up on the southwest coast of Florida. Your manager, Robin White, has asked you to investigate the possibility of developing a computer-based rental management system for Paradise Isle. To aid you in this task, White has secured the services of Daryl Simmons, a computer consultant, who will provide you with the information you need to purchase a computer system.

Today is May 12. Initially, you were to report your findings about the proposed computer system to Robin White in late June. This morning, however, you received a phone call from White, informing you that the opening date for Paradise Isle has been moved up to June 12, and your written report, including recommendations, is needed immediately. White also said that you must be specific in your recommendations, including which computer, printer, terminals, and software you would choose, and your justification for these decisions. Also, you should discuss any other factors that you feel are important to the computerization issue. White closed by saying that, due to time constraints, your report would be submitted to Jan Marshall, President of Paradise Resorts, Int'l., and you will not have any time to revise your report.

On the following pages are a series of items that have been gathered to assist you in writing your report. These include general information about the Paradise Isle resort complex and rental office, as well as specific information from Simmons pertaining to computerization of the office.

Your task in this exercise is to read through the material provided and prepare a written report for Robin White, outlining your specific recommendations and justifications regarding rental office computerization. Write your report on the pages directly following the related materials.

Figure 3.1 Paradise Resorts, Int'l. Organizational Chart

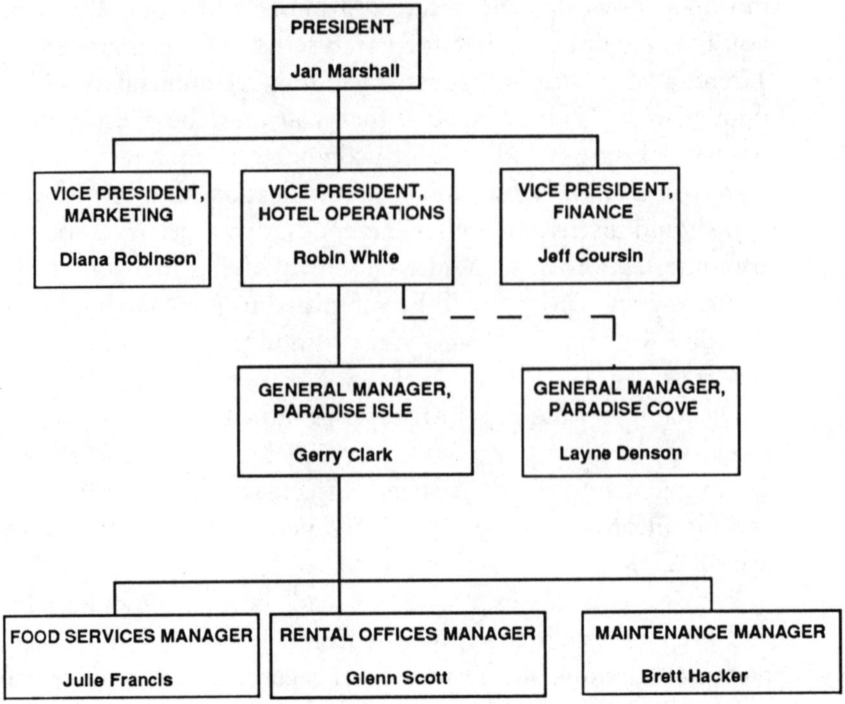

Figure 3.2   Paradise Isle

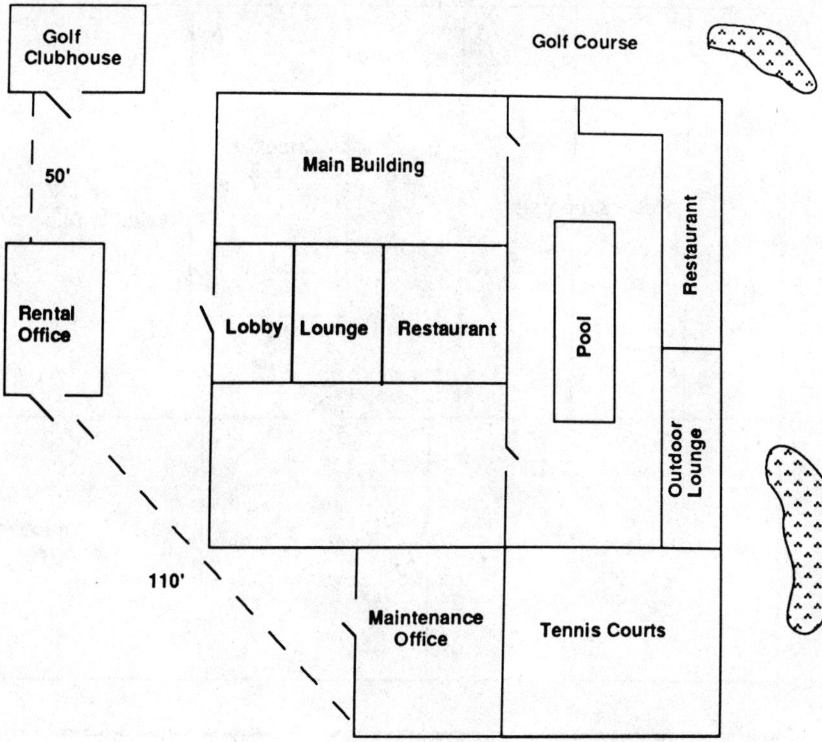

Figure 3.3   Office Layout

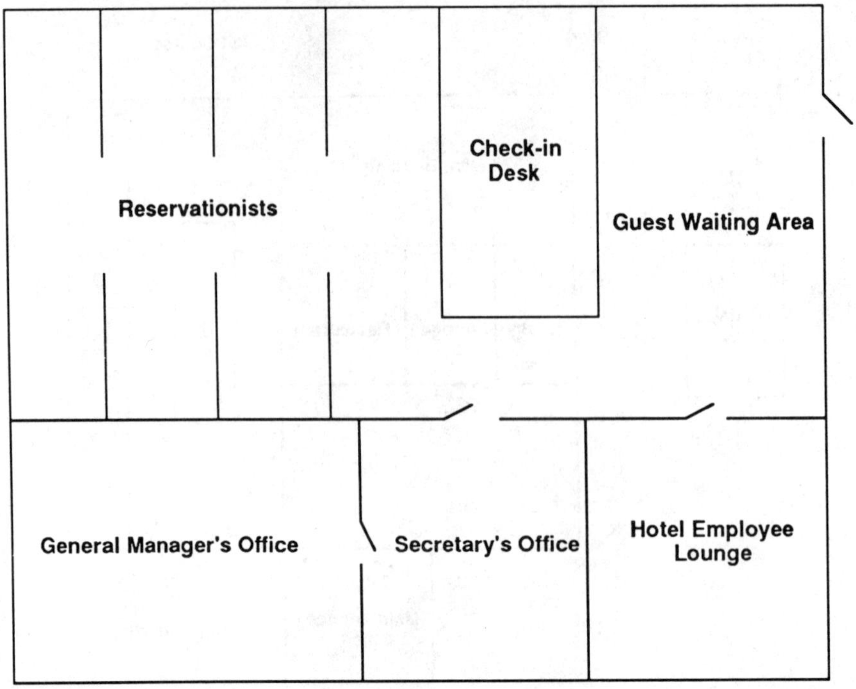

Item 3.1

Weekly Rate Structure

Room Type	Season		
	Summer	Fall/Winter	Spring
1 Bedroom	$275	$550	$400
1 Bedroom Pool View	300	600	450
2 Bedroom	325	650	500
2 Bedroom Pool View	350	700	550
3 Bedroom	375	800	650
3 Bedroom Pool View	400	800	650
Penthouse Suite	450	900	750

Item 3.2

Daryl Simmons
Computer Consulting, Inc.
196 Gregory Drive
Tampa, Florida 33613

May 12

Dear Computer Vendor:

I have been hired by Paradise Isle to investigate the computerization of their rental management system.

Paradise Isle is a luxury resort complex scheduled to open in Fort Myers Beach, Florida, on June 12. The complex consists of 600 guest rooms, two restaurants, one indoor lounge, one poolside lounge, an 18-hole golf course, and 12 lighted tennis courts.

I would appreciate your forwarding any information about computer equipment and programs you offer that would meet our needs. I have been authorized to spend $75,000 to complete this task. I look forward to hearing from you soon.

Sincerely,

Daryl Simmons

Daryl Simmons

Item 3.3

Daryl Simmons
Computer Consulting, Inc.
196 Gregory Drive
Tampa, Florida 33613

May 9

Gerry Clark
Paradise Isle
3984 Viewside Highway
Fort Myers Beach, FL 33231

Dear Gerry,

Regarding your plans to computerize your rental management operation, I have completed the detailed phase of my analysis. Based on interviews with you and your staff, as well as my own investigation, I have compiled the following information for your review.

System Objectives:

To provide the most efficient and effective service to our guests.

System Requirements:

1. Paradise Isle expects 98% of the 600 units to be occupied during the winter months; fall and spring = 75%; and summer = 50%.
2. Rental rates depend on the season, room size, and view from the room.
3. System must be able to provide immediate information on unit availability, number of units available by category, current infor-

mation on occupancies, expected departures, and a list of expected arrivals by date.

4. Through cash register terminals, the system must keep track of all payments and charges for each guest, including room rental fees, restaurant and lounge bills, and recreation fees. The system will also generate an itemized printed billing statement.

5. System must provide a confirmation number for each guest at the time the reservation is made. Advanced reservations will be cancelled after seven days if a deposit is not received.

6. System must provide housekeeping with current information on occupancies and departures.

7. A communication line is needed between housekeeping and the rental agency so that housekeeping can update the system when rooms are ready for occupancy or when rooms have been damaged.

8. System must provide the Finance Department with monthly reports detailing revenues from room rentals and all other guest charges.

9. Management would like to link the system to an accounts payable system in the future, for billing purposes.

10. Within the next two years, it is expected that 400 rooms and a third dining room will be added to the complex.

11. Rental office will staff five full-time reservationists, and one clerical.

12. Cash register terminals will be used in the golf clubhouse, tennis clubhouse, restaurants, lounges, and rental office to record all transactions.

Sincerely,

Daryl Simmons

Daryl Simmons

Item 3.4

Computer Comparison Table

Features	Compuquik 2572	TRJ 2220	MANGO 3730
Speed (transactions/sec)	50 per second	100 per second	100 per second
Capacity	Will handle all functions; up to 1000 rooms	Will handle all functions; up to 1200 rooms	Will handle all functions; up to 800 rooms
Capacity expandable?	Yes	No	Yes
Maximum # of terminals (cash register and data entry) that can be connected	23	15	21
Maximum distance terminals can be from computer without extra equipment	40 ft.	200 ft.	175 ft.
Computer languages that can be used	COBOL, PASCAL, FORTRAN, BASIC	COBOL, PASCAL, BASIC	COBOL, FORTRAN, BASIC
Printers that can be used with computer	Any	Any	MANGO series
Space requirement	150 sq. ft.	120 sq. ft.	160 sq. ft.
Special installation requirements	Special air conditioning; separate power supply	Special air conditioning; separate power supply	Special air conditioning; reinforced floor

Earliest installation date	July 15	July 31	July 22
Cost of computer	$51,250	$48,500	$55,000
Estimated cost of maintenance	$4,250/yr	$5,000/yr	$2,000/yr

Item 3.5

Printer Comparison Table

Features	MANGO 3800	HIMAJU 9333	Exuprint 2320
Speed	2 documents/ minute	10 documents/ minute	8 documents/ minute
Quality of print	Superior	Average	Below average
Computers it can be used with	Any	Compuquik, TRJ	Compuquik, TRJ
Average time to change paper from report forms to bill forms	2.5 minutes	1.75 minutes	5 minutes
Cost	$7,000	$6,500	$6,000
Maintenance cost	$1,200/yr	$1,150/yr	$1,000/yr

Item 3.6   Software Fact Sheet

1. ASTRORENT Package
   a. Manufacturer = TRJ
   b. Computer language = COBOL
   c. Training = Vendor will train staff at no additional cost.
   d. Cost = $10,000
   e. Maintenance cost = $500/yr.
   f. Comments: Comes highly recommended by other rental agencies; can be easily linked to an accounts payable system at a later date.

2. HOTEL MANAGER Package
   a. Manufacturer = Micro Business Software, Inc.
   b. Computer language = PASCAL
   c. Training = Vendor will train staff at no additional cost.
   d. Cost = $8,500
   e. Maintenance cost = $500/yr.
   f. Comments: Brand new—bugs may not be worked out, but Micro Business has a good reputation. Would require extra programs to link to an accounts payable system in the future; seems very easy to learn.

3. Develop Programs In-house
   a. Programs will be written by Daryl Simmons.
   b. Computer language = COBOL
   c. Training = Will be conducted by Daryl Simmons.
   d. Cost = $12,500
   e. Maintenance cost = $1,000/yr.
   f. Comments: Will take six months to write all the programs; can tailor the programs to the exact needs of the rental office. Training will definitely be done by someone familiar with the system.

Item 3.7   Data Entry and Cash Register Terminals Fact Sheet

1. MANGO Terminals
    a. Manufacturer = MANGO
    b. Comments: Data entry terminal will allow for contrasting video which makes data entry easier; they are compatible with any computer. Cash register terminals are adequate but may be complicated to learn.
    c. Cost = $950/terminal
    d. Maintenance cost = $100/yr.

2. Visual Designs Terminals
    a. Manufacturer = Video Displays, Inc.
    b. Comments: Data entry terminals cannot be used with MANGO or TRJ computers. They can be used with the Compuquik computer but will require extra equipment. Excellent quality of video; tilting screens and color graphics. Cash register terminals are easy to use and are compatible with any computer.
    c. Cost = $850/terminal
    d. Maintenance cost = $100/yr.

Item 3.8

PARADISE ISLE
FORT MYERS BEACH
FLORIDA   PHONE: _____

CUSTOMER'S NAME _____   ROOM # _____

ADDRESS _____   PHONE # _____

ARRIVAL DATE: _____

DEPART DATE: _____

NUMBER OF GUESTS: _____

ROOM TYPE: _____

BILLING ADDRESS:

ITEMIZED CHARGES

DATE	REFERENCE NO.	DESCRIPTION	CHARGES/CREDIT

We hope your stay at Paradise Isle was enjoyable. Thank you.

REPORT FORM

THE ANALYZER TEST

On the following pages you will find 43 statements. These statements refer to the recommendations you have just made in your report and the reasons for them. Put a check mark by the statements that describe what you saw and what you did. You may refer back to your report as you see fit. Please be as accurate as possible in regard to what you saw and what you did. If you did not see, or do, what a particular statement refers to, *do not* put a check mark next to that statement.

___ 1. Did you consider that the Compuquik computer would require extra equipment to hook up terminals in the tennis and golf clubhouses?

___ 2. Did you consider that the computer will not fit in the existing office space?

___ 3. Did you consider that the computer will need special equipment built into the room in which it is placed (i.e., special air conditioning, a separate power supply, and/or a reinforced floor)?

___ 4. Did you realize that the budget is limited to $75,000?

___ 5. Did you realize that you had to have cash register terminals in the lounges, restaurants, and recreational areas?

___ 6. Did you consider that the printer must be able to handle preprinted forms (i.e., financial reports and guest bills)?

___ 7. Did you consider that housekeeping required their own terminal to update the system and to receive daily information?

___ 8. Did you consider that different reports and bills will be printed?

___ 9. Did you realize that the ability to link the system to an accounts payable system in the future was a factor in the decision?

___10. Did you realize that the ability of the computer to expand was a factor in the decision?

___11. Did you realize that at least seven data entry terminals and eight cash register terminals would be needed when the resort opens?

___12. Did you realize that for any of the computers the speed would be more than sufficient?

___13. Did you consider that the MANGO would require expansion within the next two years?

___14. Did you consider that the TRJ already has the maximum number of terminals connected to it?

___15. Did you consider that you have to buy a MANGO printer if you buy a MANGO computer?

___16. Did you realize that none of the computers could be installed on time?

___17. Did you recommend that an interim rental system be set up until the computer system could be installed?

___18. Did you consider that computer cost differences were not significant enough to play a major part in your decision?

___19. Did you consider that the annual maintenance fees on the MANGO are less than one half of the other two computers?

___20. Did you consider that Visual Designs' cash register terminals could be used with any computer?

___21. Did you consider that the MANGO printer speed was much slower than the speed of the other two printers?

___22. Did you consider that the quality of print on the Exuprint was below average?

___23. Did you consider the time to change the type of paper in your decision?

___24. Did you consider that printer cost differences were not significant enough to play a major role in your decision?

___25. Did you consider that printer maintenance cost differences were not significant enough to play a major role in your decision?

___26. Did you consider that data entry is easier on the MANGO terminals?

___27. Did you mention in your report that you had to exceed the $75,000 budget?

___28. Did you realize that time would not permit development of an in-house software package?

___29. Did you realize that it was not cost effective to develop an in-house software package?

___30. Did you consider which computer each of the software packages would run on?

___31. Did you consider that the HOTEL MANAGER package would require extra programs to link to an accounts payable system in the future?

____32. Did you consider that HOTEL MANAGER would be easy for the reservationists to use?

____33. Did you consider that there is a potential for problems in HOTEL MANAGER because it is brand new?

____34. Did you consider that ASTRORENT was used successfully by other rental agencies?

____35. Did you consider that ASTRORENT could be linked to an accounts payable system without any additional programs?

____36. Did you consider that you didn't need to purchase the data entry terminals and the cash register terminals from the same vendor?

____37. Did you choose the ASTRORENT or HOTEL MANAGER software packages?

____38. Did you choose the HIMAJU printer?

____39. Did you consider that Visual Designs' data entry terminals required extra equipment for use with Compuquik?

____40. Did you consider that Visual Designs' data entry terminals cannot be used with the TRJ or MANGO computer?

____41. Did you choose the Compuquik computer?

____42. Did you choose the MANGO data entry terminals?

____43. Did you choose the Visual Designs cash register terminals?

Scoring the Analyzer Test

1. Add up all of the statements that you have checked. Give yourself one point for each. Give yourself one additional point for each of the following statements you checked: 2, 14, 17, 27, 36, 38, 41. (In other words, these statements earn double credit.) The sum can range from 0 to 50.
2. Write the sum in the space below.

My score on the Analyzer Test is ————————————————————— .

Calculating and Interpreting Your Analyzer mq

1. Write your score again here ———————————————————— .
2. Calculate your mq by dividing your score by 50, and then multiplying by 100. Place your answer directly below.*

$$\frac{\text{My total score}}{50} \times 100 = \text{————} \text{ Analyzer mq.}$$

Interpretation of mq

An mq of at least 75 indicates satisfactory performance with respect to the attribute being measured. It essentially means that you earned at least 75 percent of the total possible score. This 75 percent level associated with satisfactory performance is based upon our collective experience with thousands of people taking managerial/supervisory attribute tests. As your mq approaches 100, it becomes more and more exceptional. If your mq is in the 90's, you would find yourself in approximately the top 10 percent of the test takers. With an mq in the

---

* Round off the result to the nearest whole number. Your mq can range from 0 to 100.

80's, this would place you in the top 30 percent of test takers, and an mq of 75 would mean you were in the top 50 percent of test takers. An mq of below 75 would put you in the bottom 50 percent of test takers.

Developmentally speaking, any mq of below 75 would indicate an attribute in need of development. This will be discussed in further detail in Chapter 9.

CHAPTER 4

The Counselor

The Counselor demonstrates behaviors associated with the ability to develop effective interpersonal relationships. Included in this category are establishing rapport, listening attentively, and displaying sensitivity to others. In addition, the good Counselor is available to others when the need arises, demonstrates concern for their problems and an openness to their views and opinions, and encourages them to express their ideas and feelings. Along with these factors, a good Counselor helps others to think things through, discusses problems objectively, and presents feedback without damaging the others' self-esteem.

In this chapter you will find three tests designed to help you assess your own Counselor attribute.

Instructions and Test Materials

For the purpose of this exercise, you are to consider yourself Terry Haines, the newly appointed Manager of the Residential Planning Division in the Western Power and Light Company. Today is Monday, April 23, and this is your second week on the job. Your predecessor, Jan Bennett, resigned about one month ago due to health reasons. Between the time that Jan left and you took over, Dale Kinsey, the Director of Production Planning and the individual to whom you report, was the Acting Manager of Residential Planning.

As Manager of the Residential Planning Division (within the Production Planning Department), you are responsible for monitoring and forecasting power usage trends for residential customers so that WPL can correctly anticipate future power needs. Several Residential Forecasting Supervisors, who report directly to you, are responsible for monitoring the trends and projecting future needs for specific geographic territories within the province. Several forecasters and analysts are assigned to each of the Residential Forecasting Supervisors.

During the time that Dale Kinsey was Acting Manager of Residential Planning, he discovered a situation that requires immediate attention. The problem concerns one of your Residential Forecasting Supervisors, Pat Eaton. Recently, Pat has had some performance problems. He has been a Residential Forecasting Supervisor for six months. Prior to being selected for that position, Pat was a forecaster for four years. As a forecaster, he possessed excellent technical skills, was very thorough, and typically worked long hours. However, Pat's work as a supervisor has been mixed.

What follows is a summary of the information contained in Pat Eaton's personnel file. You should review and use this material to prepare for a discussion with Pat Eaton.

1. *A Memo from Dale Kinsey.* As a result of certain performance problems, Dale Kinsey (while Acting Manager) set up a meeting with Pat. However, since you are now in charge of the Residential Planning Division, Dale has written you a memo asking you to meet with Pat to discuss the problems.

   The memo also states that there have been some problems with missed deadlines coming from Pat Eaton's group, and that there have been some grumblings from Pat's subordinates concerning Pat's style of supervision.

2. *A memo from an employee in another department.* The memo extends his sincere thanks for the recent assistance provided to him by Pat Eaton. It seems Pat provided him with a two- to three-page

"white paper" regarding residential construction projections for a new subdivision.

In only two days, Pat pulled together detailed information directly related to future residential growth. In addition, Pat prepared overheads and handouts for the meeting attendees and presented an excellent overview to the group.

3. *A memo from a forecaster who reports to Pat.* The memo explains that Pat instituted a new "policy" within the group that he believes hinders rather than enhances productivity within the unit.

The policy outlines a new review process for any reports going outside the group. Essentially, all outgoing reports must be on Pat's desk five days prior to the send-out date for review. The subordinate feels five days is unreasonable since lead time is often very short, particularly when unexpected needs must be accommodated. In addition, it is felt that the five-day review process is demeaning to the more experienced forecasters, many of whom have been with WPL for more than 10 years and are fully capable of providing "clean" reports on their own.

This issue had been discussed with Pat but nothing was ever resolved. Pat was not very understanding and didn't listen to the concerns. Instead, he stated that the responsibility for everything that went out of the department rested with the supervisor. If the report looked bad, then the supervisor looked bad. Therefore, Pat wants to conduct a very detailed review and perform extensive editing on all reports.

4. *A memo from the director of another department.* The memo complains that a report was three weeks late, and that he was not notified of the delay until two days before the original due date. However, the final report did provide the information needed, plus a lot of superfluous material.

5. *A letter from Bob Brown, manager of another department.* The letter states that he asked for a three-year consumption report and Pat provided him with a five-year consumption report. This made

the report a week late and actually contained more information than was necessary.

6. *A memo from the manager of another department.* The department has a close working relationship with the Residential Planning Department, and often both groups work on joint projects together. The memo states that recently there have been several complaints coming from the forecasters and analysts working in Pat Eaton's group.

Basically, many of the senior people in Residential Planning complain about how Pat insists on going over their reports with a fine-tooth comb. They contend that the revisions made by Pat are extensive, and that the changes reflect personal preference and writing style rather than significant technical content. Many of the employees have the attitude that "you just can't please Pat no matter what you produce."

However, many of the more junior people seem to welcome the extensive comments and detailed feedback that Pat likes to provide.

7. *A project overview report.* The report shows that for the last two months there have been many late project reports coming from Pat Eaton's unit, and not the other units. The report also shows that Pat Eaton has responsibility for more project reports than the other supervisors in the department.

8. *A summary of a conversation between one of Pat's forecasters and your predecessor.* The forecaster has only been with WPL for a few months; however, he already feels like part of the "family"—thanks mainly to Pat Eaton. In the short time he's been at WPL, he has learned a great deal and feels as though he is making a significant contribution to the company. Pat Eaton has been instrumental in this development and deserves a great deal of credit.

The summary also states that Pat always took the time to review the forecaster's work in great detail and spent considerable time going over with him the revisions and the rationale for them, which helped him learn a good deal about the job in a short period of time. "I know that this is the way that Pat deals with all of the people in our group and I am sure that we all benefit from Pat's extensive input and feedback. It has helped me immeasurably and has greatly facilitated my transition from school to the real world. I look forward to continuing my development under the leadership of Pat Eaton and anticipate a long and prosperous career at WPL."

9. *A memo from the director of another department.* The memo deals with a report that is being returned to Pat's unit for revisions. Although the report is very well written and demonstrates considerable effort, as it stands it is too lengthy to pass out to committee members. They simply will not read such a long report. At most, a 10- to 15-page report could contain all of the required information. This report is 60 pages long and is much more detailed than is needed. There is a significant amount of noncritical information that should be deleted from the report.

10. *Indications of family concerns.* There are signs that Pat is having problems at home with his children. These personal problems have had a negative effect on Pat's attitude recently and on his dealings with his subordinates.

The Counselor test has three parts: 11 simulated discussions, the 5 elements of a good counseling session, and 20 multiple-choice questions. In Counselor Test I you will be discussing several issues with Pat Eaton concerning the performance problems outlined above. For each issue regarding Pat's performance, you are provided first with what you initially would have said to Pat regarding the particular issue. Next, you are provided with Pat's reply to your initial comment. At this point you will be asked to provide a written response to Pat's reply that reflects how you would deal with the particular issue. This sequence (your initial comment, Pat's reply, and your written response) will be followed until all issues have been dealt with and simulates an actual discussion that might occur between you and a hypothetical subordinate. The issues are related to one another and some have more than one comment-reply-response sequence.

In Counselor Test II, you will be asked to write down your responses to 24 questions. The questions focus on the five elements of an effective counseling session: establishing and maintaining rapport; listening to others; displaying sensitivity to others; eliciting ideas, feelings, and perceptions from others; and presenting feedback.

In Counselor Test III, you will be asked to respond to a series of multiple-choice questions aimed at measuring your counseling skills, again focusing on your interactions with Pat Eaton. By responding carefully in Counselor Tests I and II, you will ensure that you choose the best response to each question in Counselor Test III.

COUNSELOR TEST I

1. Initiating the discussion.

Your Comment: "Hello, Pat, how has everything been going lately?"

Pat's Reply: "I feel like things have been going quite well, especially during the past couple of months."

Your Response:

_____

_____

_____

_____

_____

_____

2. *Issue:* Decline in performance.

Your Comment: "Pat, I notice that you have been having some performance problems lately."

Pat's Reply: "Oh really, I was under the impression that everything was going well. I'm surprised that's what you want to talk to me about."

Your Response:

_____

_____

_____

_____

_____

_____

3. *Issue:* Complaint about the new five-day review policy.

Your Comment: "I noticed that you instituted a new policy within your group that requires all outgoing reports to be submitted to you five days before their due date. Don't you think that's unreasonable?"

Pat's Reply: "Well, I feel that I need that much time in order to polish the final reports so that they shine. I also want those reports to be the very highest quality possible because they reflect on me, and in order to ensure that everything is thoroughly covered, I need the five days."

Your Response:

_____

_____

_____

_____

_____

_____

4. *Issue:* Complaint about the new five-day review policy.

Your Comment: "Don't you think perhaps the policy might be demeaning to, or shows lack of trust in, the more experienced personnel?"

Pat's Reply: "Well, they still make occasional mistakes and the review is my only means of quality control. I really feel that the final reports should be the highest quality possible, and I'd feel uncomfortable letting average reports go out."

Your Response:

_____

_____

_____

_____

_____

_____

5. *Issue:* Complaint about the new five-day review policy.

Your Comment: "Don't you think perhaps the five-day review period is more beneficial for the junior (i.e., newer) employees than for the senior employees?"

Pat's Reply: "Well, I hadn't thought of that but I'd be concerned that differential treatment between experienced and less-experienced employees might be seen as unfair, and I really want to maintain harmony in the group."

Your Response:

_____

_____

_____

_____

_____

_____

6. *Issue:* Report that was three weeks late.

Your Comment: "Why was one of your reports three weeks late?"

Pat's Reply: "I needed extra time to collect additional data so that I could produce a highly comprehensive report."

Your Response:

_____

_____

_____

_____

_____

7. *Issue:* Report that was three weeks late.

Your Comment: "Was the report late because of the extra information that was included in the report?"

Pat's Reply: "I was only trying to do a comprehensive and thorough job. I would rather provide too much information than too little, and actually, the user can read only what is important and ignore what is not important."

Your Response:

_____

_____

_____

_____

_____

8. *Issue:* Five-year consumption report provided to Bob Brown.

Your Comment: "Why did you give Bob Brown a five-year consumption report when he only asked for a three-year forecast?"

Pat's Reply: "I thought this kind of thoroughness would be much more useful to Bob Brown, and I wanted the report to be looked upon as the best possible."

Your Response:

_____

_____

_____

_____

_____

_____

9. *Issue:* Complaints from senior staff in Pat's unit.

Your Comment: "Did you know that some of your more senior staff have been complaining about your review of their work? They say that you go over their work with a fine-tooth comb and most of the time just focus on their writing style."

Pat's Reply: "This is my method for controlling the quality of reports that leave my office, and I always strive for top quality. Besides, my writing style and format have worked extremely well in the past and I'm just trying to perpetuate a good practice."

Your Response:

_____

_____

_____

_____

_____

_____

10. *Issue:* Project overview showing late reports for the past two months.

Your Comment: "Did you know that you're the only supervisor that has been turning in late reports over the past two months?"

Pat's Reply: "All I wanted to do was make sure that the reports were comprehensive because of the importance of those projects. I did include additional information, but I thought I was doing it for the good of the company. And the reason that I'm the only one who has late reports is because I have a lot more reports to finish than the other supervisors, and I've been working overtime to finish them."

Your Response:

_____

_____

_____

_____

_____

_____

11. *Issue:* Report that was returned because it is too long and will not be read.

Your Comment: "Why did you submit a 60-page report when only 10 or 15 pages were needed?"

Pat's Reply: "It's because the committee meeting that I prepared the report for was an important one and I simply wanted to do a bang-up job because of all of the visibility associated with this project. I'm surprised the committee members wouldn't read it because there was a lot of good information in the report."

Your Response:

_____

COUNSELOR TEST II

Now that you have thought about and written down your responses during a discussion with Pat, we will turn to some specific aspects of the Counselor attribute. Write down your answers to the following questions, which deal with the five elements of good counseling discussion.

In *establishing and maintaining rapport*, a comfortable relationship with another, or others, is achieved. The ability to establish rapport is a major part of the counselor's work. Use the information you reviewed to answer questions 1–5 in the following section.

1. One of the first steps in conducting a meeting is establishing rapport. Knowing some personal information about the person with whom you are meeting will show that you are interested in that person. It will also help make that person more receptive to your comments and will promote openness and honesty. What do you know about Pat that can help you establish rapport?

   _____

   _____

   _____

   _____

   _____

2. How would you utilize information to help establish rapport with Pat during your meeting?

   _____

   _____

   _____

_____

_____

_____

3. How would you begin to deal with Pat's performance problems as you perceive them and still maintain rapport?

_____

_____

_____

_____

_____

4. How would you best position some of the complaints about Pat to further establish rapport with Pat at this meeting?

_____

_____

_____

_____

5. How could you specifically use the commendations of Pat's performance to maintain rapport with Pat and still accomplish what you wish to accomplish regarding Pat's negative performance?

_____

_____

_____

———————————————————————————————————

———————————————————————————————————

In *listening to others*, you let the speaker know that his or her message has been heard, understood, and respected. Use the information you have reviewed to answer questions 6–9 in the following section.

6. During your meeting with Pat, what type of body language could you use to show that you are interested in what Pat is saying?

———————————————————————————————————

———————————————————————————————————

———————————————————————————————————

———————————————————————————————————

———————————————————————————————————

7. How would you make sure that Pat knows you have heard and understood his message when he answers your various questions?

———————————————————————————————————

———————————————————————————————————

———————————————————————————————————

———————————————————————————————————

———————————————————————————————————

8. When Pat states that the reason for the five-day review policy is so that the reports will be of the very highest quality possible, how could you indicate respect for that message, and at the same time a need for the overall situation to change?

_____

_____

_____

_____

_____

9. Summarize what you would say to Pat to indicate a sympathetic attitude toward his increased work load?

_____

_____

_____

_____

_____

In *displaying sensitivity to others,* you indicate by your actions a consideration for the feelings and needs of others. Included here are such things as being concerned with their well-being, their problems, and their right to privacy. Use the information you reviewed to answer questions 10–14 in the following section.

10. When giving feedback to Pat, how could you couch the feedback and disagreement in constructive and polite terms?

_____

_____

_____

_____

_____

11. If Pat were to claim that you were too new in the position to be able
to understand the whole situation, how would you deal with the
comment?

_____

_____

_____

_____

_____

12. How would you move to resolve the problems with the morale on
Pat's staff? Specifically, what would you say to Pat or do to begin this
part of the conversation?

_____

_____

_____

_____

13. What would you say if Pat were to indicate that he might not be cut
out to be a supervisor and maybe should be transferred to another
department?

_____

_____

_____

_____

_____

_____

14. What other follow-up actions or plans would you take to ensure that the problems with Pat were resolved, and how would you communicate this to Pat?

_____

_____

_____

_____

_____

_____

In *eliciting ideas, feelings, and perceptions from others,* you allow them to participate in discussions and in the decision-making process when it affects them. This is accomplished by creating an atmosphere that allows others to express themselves freely and honestly. Use the information you reviewed to answer questions 15–19 in the following section.

15. There is a memo that states that there is a morale problem with some of Pat's subordinates. What could you say to Pat to elicit Pat's perceptions and ideas regarding this problem? Explain how your comment might affect Pat's response.

_____

_____

_____

———————————————————————

———————————————————————

16. Pat's five-day review policy appears to be upsetting some of the more experienced employees in the work unit. Pat does not appear to be aware of the problems that this is causing. How could you encourage Pat to think about the effect of this policy?

———————————————————————

———————————————————————

———————————————————————

———————————————————————

———————————————————————

17. Many of Pat's reports have been late over the past few months. How would you bring up this issue with Pat?

———————————————————————

———————————————————————

———————————————————————

———————————————————————

18. Pat has spent too much time on one of the reports. The report contains much more information than was called for. What would you say that would allow you to discuss this issue in a way that will not threaten Pat.

———————————————————————

———————————————————————

_____

_____

_____

_____

19. What can you say, with regard to any of the problems or issues covered in the discussion, that will indicate that you value and will give serious consideration to Pat's opinions?

_____

_____

_____

_____

_____

_____

In *presenting feedback effectively,* you make sure the person receiving the feedback feels positive about the information presented and is encouraged to grow. Use the information you reviewed to answer questions 20–24 in the following section.

20. What feedback would you provide to Pat regarding your expectations for future performance?

_____

_____

_____

_____

_____

_____

21. What reasons are there for involving Pat in the discussion regarding the performance problems, and how would you do this?

——————————————————————————————————

——————————————————————————————————

——————————————————————————————————

——————————————————————————————————

——————————————————————————————————

22. Specifically describe what you would say to Pat to guard against Pat losing any self-esteem or respect.

——————————————————————————————————

——————————————————————————————————

——————————————————————————————————

——————————————————————————————————

——————————————————————————————————

23. What would you say to make the critical issues regarding Pat's performance less personal and more business related?

——————————————————————————————————

——————————————————————————————————

——————————————————————————————————

——————————————————————————————————

——————————————————————————————————

24. How would you indicate to Pat that the performance problems were significant and that performance needed to improve in the future. How would you also indicate a willingness to help with the improvement so that the situation will be minimally threatening?

————————————————————————————————————

————————————————————————————————————

————————————————————————————————————

————————————————————————————————————

————————————————————————————————————

————————————————————————————————————

COUNSELOR TEST III

We will now have you answer 20 multiple-choice questions that pertain to the information you reviewed with respect to Pat Eaton's performance problems. As you answer the questions, consider your responses in Counselor Tests I and II and use them as the basis for your answers. For each question, choose the one statement that best answers the question. You may refer back to the summary of information as you do the test.

____ 1. In establishing rapport with Pat, what background information would you use at the start of your meeting?
   a. Pat is important enough to the organization that your boss has requested you meet with him.
   b. Pat's performance has been declining only for a few months, and has been better in the past.
   c. He produces very good reports and has strong skills in the area of being an independent supervisor.
   d. A letter of commendation from a manager in another department has been received as a result of Pat's hard work.

____ 2. How would you use the background information to help accomplish your goal of establishing rapport with Pat and solving the problems?
   a. Question why Pat cannot seem to get all of his reports done on time since he gets some of them done on time.
   b. Express confidence in Pat based on his positive qualities, pointing out the problem areas and involving him in planning the overall strategy to change.
   c. Discuss job changes more in line with his perceived areas of strength.
   d. Use the positive qualities displayed in some problem areas to further question Pat as to why they are not displayed in other problem areas.

___ **3.** How could you begin to deal with some of the negative aspects of Pat's performance and still maintain rapport?

    a. After dealing with the positive aspects of Pat's performance, move to the negative aspects and indicate the absolute necessity for change.

    b. Solicit his input on some of the problem areas, making sure the problems are dealt with in specific detail.

    c. Minimize the importance of the negative aspects of his performance by opening the discussion with the fact that it was someone else who thought he should be talked to and not you.

    d. Turn some of the problems into compliments by praising him for the quality of the reports that he produces.

___ **4.** In what way could you specifically use the commendation by the other manager to best advantage in furthering what you wish to accomplish as well as establishing rapport?

    a. Explore job changes that would take advantage of his good presentation and preparation skills.

    b. Explore why he appears to be successful at doing some things well but is having trouble with others.

    c. Suggest that some of the skills he appears to have in regard to getting along with peers be applied internally with his subordinates.

    d. Suggest he use the same strategy to plan the timing of his reports as he did for preparing his presentation.

___ **5.** What would you do in your meeting with Pat to have your body language indicate interest in what he is saying?

    a. Lean forward and look intently at Pat.

    b. Lean back in a relaxed posture and look intently at Pat.

    c. Stare thoughtfully at the ceiling, indicating you are giving thought to what is being said.

    d. Tap a pencil to punctuate his points and to indicate you are receiving his message.

___ **6.** How would you make sure that Pat knows you have heard and understood his message when he answers your various questions?

a. State, "I understand what you are saying."

b. Nod your head to indicate understanding.

c. Paraphrase, or reword, what he said.

d. Repeat exactly, word for word, what he has said.

_____ 7. How would you perceive Pat's lack of concern for getting reports done on time, and how would you deal with it?

a. Pat spends too much time reviewing work, thus lessening his overall chances of getting work done on time. You must get him to stop reviewing work unnecessarily.

b. Pat's subordinates aren't giving him the support he needs, so he has to do most of the work himself. Pat has to coach his subordinates so that they will be more cooperative.

c. Recent personal problems have caused delays in his work; you must begin to explore these problems further so that he might be able to work enough to get the reports done on time.

d. Pat is not happy with his lack of recognition for the things he does well, and this is becoming a major issue; you must deal with it before other things can improve.

_____ 8. How would you explore further the extent to which Pat's personal problems might be interfering with work?

a. "Pat, it's none of my business, but I am certainly available to help you think through some personal issues that may be interfering with your work."

b. "Pat, I feel a good manager has to get involved with his employees at both a personal and work level. If there are any problems bothering you of a personal nature, you should share them with me."

c. "Pat, I've noticed a few indications in your file of some personal problems which may be affecting your work. Why don't you share some of those with me?"

d. "Pat, everyone has personal problems from time to time which may interfere with their work. If you're comfortable sharing those with me, I'd be glad to listen and help you in any way I can."

___ **9.** If Pat were to indicate you were too new to truly appreciate his situation, how would you respond?

    a. "Even though I'm new, I am basically responsible for the performance of my entire section. We need to start somewhere by making me more knowledgeable about the situation."

    b. "I realize I'm new, and we can leave many of the problems until I have some additional opportunity to gather information, but there are some things with which we need to deal."

    c. "The kinds of problems I see us dealing with can be dealt with by someone who is new because they are organizationally related and really quite clear cut."

    d. "Even though I'm new, your personal problems as well as the organizational ones can be looked at objectively, even more so because of the fact I'm new."

___ **10.** What would you say to Pat to begin the process of resolving the morale problems with his senior subordinates?

    a. "I want to sit down with you and some of your senior subordinates to begin to talk through the problems."

    b. "I want you to meet with some of your subordinates separately and try to come up with a plan you both agree on to resolve the problems."

    c. "I'm going to meet with some of your subordinates and gather some additional information about the problems. Then, we can get together to discuss things further."

    d. "If we can deal successfully with some of your personal problems first, then we can get together with everyone and look more clearly at the organizational ones. So let's try to put you in a better frame of mind first."

___ **11.** What would you say to Pat if he were to indicate a desire for a different kind of job within the organization?

    a. "We can explore that certainly, and perhaps we should start with your feelings about what that job should be like."

b. "That is certainly a possibility, but we need to deal with the existing problems first, and then turn our attention to other possibilities."

c. "There are really no other kinds of jobs that would demand significantly different activities. There would still be a need to schedule and coordinate and work effectively with others. So, let's look at those problems rather than searching for alternatives."

d. "I would certainly support that, and you could go to personnel and explore the types of positions which could be possible. Then we could talk further."

___12. What further follow-up or action would you take on any of the problems, and how would you indicate this to Pat?

a. Set up a series of subsequent meetings with Pat, giving him a specific agenda for each item. Indicate to him the need to start this immediately.

b. Set up a series of subsequent meetings with Pat, and let him report on the progress of the different problems. Indicate the need to start this immediately.

c. Jointly select the most serious or important problems, and set up a subsequent meeting on these to review the progress.

d. Have Pat by himself select the most serious or important problems, and set up a subsequent meeting with him on these, to review the progress.

___13. Which statement would most likely elicit Pat's ideas, feelings, and perceptions about the complaints made by his subordinates?

a. "Your subordinates have been commenting about you, and I want to really understand your side of the issue before I act."

b. "Do you feel there are problems with any of your subordinates?"

c. "Do you feel your subordinates are justified in their criticisms of you?"

d. "There have been some problem areas between you and some of your subordinates. What are your thoughts on these issues, and what can we do to resolve them?"

——14. Which statement would best encourage Pat to think through the problems his subordinates are having with the criticisms of their work and the impact this has on the work unit?

   a. "Have you given some thought to the impact this has on your subordinates?"

   b. "Do you have any idea how this criticism upsets everyone in the department?"

   c. "Why do you think your subordinates react so negatively to your reviewing of their work?"

   d. "I know the quality of the reports coming out of your department is very good, but don't you think you should let some of your subordinates take some of the responsibility for their own work?"

——15. What can you say to Pat that will best indicate that you value, and will give serious consideration to, his opinions?

   a. "I will certainly look into what you've told me and get back to you."

   b. "Your ideas certainly have merit, and I will give them lots of thought."

   c. "Based on what you've told me, there is certainly some merit here. Let's individually think about them further and meet here next Thursday."

   d. "You're absolutely right. I'll change things as soon as I can."

——16. How would you summarize your feedback to Pat at the end of the meeting?

   a. "Pat, we've covered a great many topics that need further discussion. It seems we've agreed on the following points and actions, and we'll get back together one week from today."

   b. "Pat, there are lots of changes you need to make, but I'm sure you can do it. I look forward to working with you."

   c. "Pat, it appears that you are facing a great many problems, both personal and job related. Let's use the next meeting as an opportunity to explore all of them over time."

d. "Pat, I enjoyed talking to you. Let me follow up with some of your subordinates and see if I can resolve some of the problems. In the meantime, don't worry; we can work things out, I'm sure."

___17. How would you involve Pat in his own performance review during the discussion?
   a. "Pat, how do you see your own performance in regard to what we've agreed are your major responsibilities?"
   b. "Pat, I see your performance as weak in the following areas and strong in these areas. What do you think?"
   c. "Pat, your strengths have far exceeded your weaknesses; there are some things that need developing. What do you think those are?"
   d. "Pat, your weaknesses in some critical areas appear significant. We need to begin to work on those as soon as possible. What do you suggest?"

___18. What would you say to Pat to protect his self-esteem at the end of the discussion?
   a. "Pat, you certainly have some very important strengths and a work record that has been awfully good in the past. Let's see if we can get things back to that level again."
   b. "Pat, you certainly have developed some problems recently, but nothing that can't be overcome. Let's work on it together."
   c. "Pat, some of your personal problems are perhaps out of your control, so let's try to work on the work-related areas that have been affected."
   d. "Pat, everyone has weaknesses, so it's nothing to be ashamed of. Let's work on things together, and I'm sure it will be OK."

___19. What would you emphasize in order to make the critical issues less personal in regard to Pat's performance?
   a. Emphasize the fact that Pat's non-job-related problems are likely affecting his work.
   b. Emphasize the fact that all people have differences, and it's simply something to be worked on.

c. Emphasize the fact that Pat has many strengths as well as some weaknesses.

d. Emphasize the fact that the problems relate to decisions Pat has made under specific circumstances and are not necessarily weaknesses of his.

___**20.** How do you indicate to Pat that you will be continuously involved in the issues and make it as minimally threatening as possible, yet effective?

a. "I'll be involved in working with you and helping in any way I can. Let's meet monthly to review things."

b. "I'll be watching those problem areas we discussed, and I'll give you as much feedback as possible as to changes I see."

c. "You just report to me when you feel you need to. I'll monitor the situation by talking to your subordinates."

d. "I'll meet with you monthly to stay on top of what's going on, and you should also submit a progress report to me each month."

Scoring Counselor Test III

On the following pages are the correct answers to the multiple-choice questions. Accompanying each correct answer is a short explanation.

1. Compare your choice to the correct answer on all 20 questions. Place a check mark by each question you answered correctly. Be sure to read the explanation for the correct choice for each question.
2. Add up the check marks. The sum can range from 0 to 20.
3. Write the sum in the space below.

My score on Counselor Test III is _____ .

Correct Answers and Explanations

Q#	ANS	Explanation
___ 1.	a.	Pat is important to the organization. This is a stronger statement in creating feelings of worth in Pat than any of the others because it truly encompasses many other specifics, such as the commendation from the manager, as well as the other positive comments.
___ 2.	b.	Expressing confidence in Pat, pointing out the problem areas, and involving him in the overall strategy for change would go furthest toward establishing rapport and resolving the problems. It is too early for job changes, and the other choices have a confrontative and almost threatening aspect to them.
___ 3.	b.	Soliciting as much input as possible at the beginning will lead to the best opportunity for resolution as long as the specific details are covered. The problems are serious enough so that they shouldn't be minimized.

___ 4. d.   Pat apparently has the skills in the area of organizing and planning. He needs to realize that the skill necessary to plan his presentation could also be used to help structure the timing of his reports. As before, it is premature to consider job changes, and simple, broad suggestions would not be as effective as specific directions for action.

___ 5. a.   Leaning forward and staring intently at Pat shows greater interest in what he is saying than any of the other choices. Staring at the ceiling does not allow him to know how interested you are, nor does leaning back in a relaxed position show intense interest. Tapping a pencil could be distracting.

___ 6. c.   Paraphrasing is the best means by which you can show understanding. Repeating word for word does not indicate understanding, nor do the other choices. A demonstration of understanding comes best from rewording one's comments.

___ 7. a.   Obviously there are some underlying problems which must be explored. Perhaps personal problems are an issue, but before that assumption is explored, the basis for all the work organization issues should be dealt with.

___ 8. a.   Indicating no organizational right to know about personal problems yet availability to help and relating the personal issues to the work situation cover best what needs to be expressed. Good managers don't necessarily need to get involved in personal problems of employees but should certainly be available if needed.

_____ 9. b. The role of manager demands starting to work on the problem situation. The most effective way of handling this is to treat it as a job-related set of activities that don't necessarily benefit from the manager being new, aren't necessarily clear-cut, and cannot be left for a later time.

_____10. b. Placing the burden of initially working through problems on Pat and his subordinates is the best choice. There are enough indications of subordinate-related problems so that your doing any investigating before there is better communication and agreement among the staff would not be as effective.

_____11. b. The possibilities for changing his position should not be ruled out entirely, but certainly there are more immediate issues which must be dealt with. Changing the job at this point would not be an effective way of dealing directly with Pat's present difficulties.

_____12. c. Jointly selecting the most serious or important problems not only ensures that proper priorities are being determined, but also involves Pat in the effort, thus building up support.

_____13. d. Acknowledging that there have been problems involving some of Pat's subordinates and soliciting Pat's perceptions of the situation is the best starting point to elicit open communication. It is also best not to word such things in a way that indicates Pat is probably wrong, but also best not to place the entire blame on others.

_____14. d. Using a relatively positive subject (the quality of the reports) to have Pat examine what he does and its impact on his subordinates is the best way to open the conversation. Blaming and pointing out the negative attitudes of his subordinates will build a defensive attitude with respect to the discussion.

——15.　c.　Expressing the thought that his ideas have merit and that you will discuss them best indicates you're serious about his opinions. Setting up a specific meeting emphasizes this.

——16.　a.　Acknowledge the variety of topics covered, summarize the conclusions, and set up a subsequent time for getting back together. All other choices concerning personal problems, your resolving the problems, or simply an "I know you can do it," fall short of what needs to be accomplished.

——17.　a.　Tying Pat's performance to his responsibilities and soliciting his opinion is the best way to involve Pat in the review. It would be counterproductive to begin by stating what Dale Kinsey perceived Pat's strengths and weaknesses to be.

——18.　a.　Emphasize his previously strong record and the need to return to a more effective level of performance. This comment includes the fact that it certainly can be done.

——19.　d.　The problems are made less personal with this choice. Pat has made some bad decisions, but these are not necessarily indicative of weaknesses that go beyond those decisions. Using the word *weakness* is not as good as mentioning specifics about what should be done differently.

——20.　a.　The offer of assistance combined with specific monthly meetings is what you want to convey to Pat. Treating it as a matter of course helps to remove the threatening aspect.

Calculating and Interpreting Your Counselor mq

1. Write your score again here _____ .
2. Calculate your mq by dividing your score by 20, and then multiplying by 100. Place your answer directly below.*

$$\frac{\text{My total score}}{20} \times 100 = \underline{\hspace{2cm}} \text{ Counselor mq.}$$

Interpretation of mq

An mq of at least 75 indicates satisfactory performance with respect to the attribute being measured. It essentially means that you earned at least 75 percent of the total possible score. This 75 percent level associated with satisfactory performance is based upon our collective experience with thousands of people taking managerial/supervisory attribute tests. As your mq approaches 100, it becomes more and more exceptional. If your mq is in the 90's, you would find yourself in approximately the top 10 percent of the test takers. With an mq in the 80's, this would place you in the top 30 percent of test takers, and an mq of 75 would mean you were in the top 50 percent of test takers. An mq of below 75 would put you in the bottom 50 percent of test takers.

Developmentally speaking, any mq of below 75 would indicate an attribute in need of development. This will be discussed in further detail in Chapter 9.

* Round off the result to the nearest whole number. Your mq can range from 0 to 100.

CHAPTER 5

The Communicator

The Communicator demonstrates behaviors associated with the ability to be persuasive through either written or oral communications. Included in this category are some basic presentation skills, such as using the voice effectively, choosing a vocabulary appropriate for the audience, and using effective nonverbal accompaniments such as gestures or audiovisual aids to emphasize issues or points of discussion. Points should be organized so that conclusions flow logically. The good Communicator integrates the material around them and chooses the most effective words and phrases, whether to an audience of thousands or a single individual.

In this chapter you will find four tests designed to help you assess your own Communicator attribute.

Instructions and Information

For the purpose of this exercise, you are to consider yourself Lynn Sommers of the Starport Computer Company. You report directly to one of the regional vice presidents (RVP), who has been asked to form a committee with the other RVP's and present a recommendation for the location of a new manufacturing plant. Currently, Starport has several manufacturing facilities throughout the Midwest, manufacturing and distributing their model 70293 and 70393 computers. Last year Starport redesigned one of the older, smaller plants to test the market for a new line of computers, the model 70493. Sales on the new model have been increasing steadily. Projections show that Starport will outgrow the 70493 plant within a few years. The presentation will last approximately 30 minutes, so your boss has asked that you prepare a five-page written speech. After the presentation your boss will be required to answer questions and elaborate on the issues.

On the following pages is some information concerning the location your boss wants to propose, the other RVP's, the company, and some data on other locations. Study this information carefully before you write the speech. Here are some specific points that you will have to cover in the speech:

1. What is the best city in which to locate the plant?
2. Why are you recommending the city?
3. What are the implications of locating the plant at the proposed city?
4. Does the proposed city have the necessary resources to handle the new plant?

Riverbend, Louisiana: Detailed Report

Over the past few years, several oil refineries near Riverbend have shut down. As of the last quarter, the unemployment rate in Riverbend is high, compared to the other sites being considered. Although the availability of laborers is high, the educational level is low. Expect high training costs in this area, due to the need for remedial training, in addition to the established training program. The average hourly wage, however, is relatively low. Many young families have left the area, as indicated by the drastic reduction in public school enrollment. This may affect the availability of workers in the future. The high school dropout rate has increased from 14.3 to 27.6 percent over the past 10 years, indicating a reduction in education level of potential workers.

Labor costs, relative to companywide averages, are low in this area. It is expected that labor costs here will always be below companywide averages. The training cost, however, is considerably higher than the companywide average. This is due primarily to the low education level of the residents. Although the city and state are aggressive in their campaign efforts to increase the education level of their residents, no noticeable difference is expected in the labor pool for at least 20 years.

The federal government offers a couple of programs, in the form of partial tax waivers, designed to attract large companies into economically depressed areas. Starport will benefit greatly from these programs, because of the local economy. The state has also agreed to a partial tax waiver for Starport.

The proposed site is located just outside the downtown area. The city will widen and resurface the major roads leading to the site from nearby interstates. All necessary utilities are currently serving the surrounding areas, and the city will extend them to the proposed site.

The site is located three and a half miles from a major interstate highway, with two exits serving the area. The city will widen and resurface these roads to accommodate heavy traffic flow from employees and trucks. Based on the distance from suppliers, raw materials, shipped by truck, will cost significantly more than the companywide average.

The site is located four miles from the Mississippi River, where several ports are available for lease. Finished products can be delivered to Central and South America by ship, at a cost lower than is currently paid by the existing 70493 plant. Markets in the southern United States can be reached by truck at a lower cost, also. Markets in Europe can be reached for costs approximating the companywide averages. Costs to reach the projected markets will be slightly higher than average.

The Riverbend area is economically depressed. Many people have left the city, resulting in high availability of resale homes, and extremely low prices. The quality of public education is well below national averages. This may impact the ability to recruit management to this location. The Riverbend area is well known for its cultural opportunities, as well as its good restaurants, theaters, clubs, and other forms of entertainment.

Other Regional Vice Presidents

- **John Miles.** John is chairman of the committee. He is a strong proponent for the Riverbend location, as he is originally from Louisiana. While he doesn't know which site is being recommended, he will vote for the Riverbend location regardless.
- **Stephanie Dowden.** Stephanie will be coordinating the management recruiting efforts and is favoring Woodsdale, Indiana, which has a much higher quality of life, including education quality and quality housing availability.
- **Wally Lynton.** Wally will be most concerned with the cost of receiving raw materials. He has been with the company for 30 years and is convinced that nothing else matters except shipping costs. For this reason he is not likely to see Riverbend as a viable location.
- **Craig Deems.** Craig is the newest vice president on the committee. This will be the first issue he has voted on. He is very unfamiliar with the new plant locations. Craig has a Ph.D. in education and teaches part-time at a local university.
- **Cathy Stillwell.** Cathy is attending the meeting at the request of the president of the company. She is the plant manager of the existing computer plant and has been asked to attend in order to respond to your boss's presentation, based on her experiences with the current plant. While she will not have a vote in the final decision, she may heavily influence the committee members with her responses to the presentation.

Starport Computer Company

Starport manufactures almost all of the components for their computers from raw materials and electronics purchased throughout the United States. The computers are then assembled, and the finished products are packaged and distributed to wholesalers worldwide. The new plant will be responsible for all facets of production for the model 70493. When the new plant opens, it will assume all production for the model 70493; the existing 70493 plant will be redesigned to test another new product.

Sales for the model 70493 in Europe have been increasing steadily since the introduction of the product. It is expected that this trend will continue for several years to come, taking a larger percentage of total sales. Markets are also opening up in Canada, but the projections there are still speculative. Although current sales there are expected to remain fairly constant, the percentage of total sales will decrease. The sales in Central and South America have been strong and steady, and they are expected to remain constant, in terms of dollars. Sales are increasing slightly in the United States, with the South and Southwest showing the largest gains.

The new manufacturing plant will be the largest in the company. It will employ 2400 production personnel and 120 first-line supervisors. These positions will be filled by the local labor pool. Other management positions will be filled by management currently working at the existing 70493 plant, or recruited nationwide.

Other Possible Locations and Their Benefits

Woodsdale, Indiana	High total labor costs, few government incentives, very low transportation costs for shipping and receiving, and a high quality-of-life factor.
Taylor, Kansas	Moderate total labor costs, no government incentives to help reduce costs, moderate transportation costs, and a moderate quality-of-life factor.
Hamilton, Iowa	Moderate total labor costs, some local government incentives to help defray start-up costs, moderate transportation costs, and a very high quality-of-life factor.

| Danbury, Delaware | Low total labor costs, no government incentives, very low transportation costs for shipping and receiving, and a low quality-of-life factor. |
| Norris, New Mexico | High total labor costs, local and federal incentives to help defray ongoing costs, moderate transportation costs, and a moderate quality-of-life factor. |

The Task: Writing the Speech

Instructions for writing the speech are as follows:

1. On the next five pages, write out a presentation for your boss to read to the other regional vice presidents. Refer to the information provided earlier.
2. Be sure, as far as possible, that the recommendation covers everything.
3. The recommendation should include both the positive and negative implications of the proposed site on the company.
4. Since a final decision has not been made, you need to prepare the presentation carefully. The committee could decide to look at a location other than the one your boss wants to propose.

PRESENTATION

Summary Questions on the Written Presentation

Before proceeding with the Communicator Test, we ask that you respond to the 15 questions below on the presentation you have just written. These questions ask you to look at the speech carefully, think it through, and begin to evaluate it objectively.

Please write your response on the lines following each question.

1. Why were you writing this speech?

   _____

   _____

   _____

2. What did you wish to accomplish by writing this speech?

   _____

   _____

   _____

3. What sources of information did you use to write the speech?

   _____

   _____

   _____

4. How did you structure the information in your speech to ensure that it was organized and easy to understand, without jumping from one topic to another?

   _____

   _____

   _____

5. Who is the intended audience of the presentation, and how would their backgrounds affect the contents of the speech?

_____

_____

_____

6. From what perspective would the listeners review the speech?

_____

_____

_____

7. How familiar are the other vice presidents with the whole situation and the alternative locations?

_____

_____

_____

8. Did you avoid using superlatives, such as "absolute" and "best," to maintain impartiality? Note some examples from your speech.

_____

_____

_____

9. Did you avoid using the same words or phrases over and over? Note some examples from your speech.

_____

_____

_____

10. Did you use appropriate grammar and good paragraph construction? For example, did you make sure that each paragraph focused on only one main point and contained a topic sentence? Note some examples from your speech.

_____

_____

_____

11. Did you use an outline format or paragraph headings to help structure the presentation? Note some examples from your speech.

_____

_____

_____

12. To what extent did your speech vary from the intended objectives? (In other words, did you stick to the point?) Support your answer.

_____

_____

_____

13. After you wrote the speech, did you take time to go back and reread it, to ensure that it met the general purpose of the speech and that the style and tone were appropriate for the intended audience? What style and tone did you use in the speech?

_____

_____

_____

14. When evaluating your speech, did you look at the total number of words, making sure you did not use too many? Note some examples from your speech.

_____

_____

15. When evaluating your speech, did you use appropriate vocabulary and language, making sure you avoided technical jargon and excessively long words? Note some examples from your speech.

———————————————————————————————————————

———————————————————————————————————————

———————————————————————————————————————

The Communicator Test has four parts: written communication, oral communication, word usage, and spelling. In Communicator Test I, on written communication, you will evaluate again the speech you just wrote by reviewing your responses to the 15 questions above.

COMMUNICATOR TEST I:
WRITTEN COMMUNICATION

We would now like you to reevaluate your written presentation in the following way:

1. Review the 15 questions above and your responses to them.
2. The questions are repeated below. Following each question is a statement summarizing some pertinent points regarding the issue raised by the question—things you should have done, or should have considered doing, in your responses. Compare your responses above to these statements below. Remember, these statements are *summaries* of pertinent points. They do not cover everything; therefore, you will have to look critically at your responses to determine whether you have met the requirements for a satisfactory rating of each question. Be objective.
3. Place a check mark beside the question if you feel that your written response (above) was a satisfactory one, based on the accompanying statement. In other words, did you think it through carefully?
4. Add up the check marks and write the sum on the line following the questions and statements below.

____ 1. Why were you writing this speech?
Statements need to be made about the overall purpose for the presentation. Some examples might concern possible cities for the new plant location, information on the computer market, or facts about the new product.

____ 2. What did you wish to accomplish by writing this speech?
A specific goal for the speech might be to address the recommended location for the new plant, as well as the implications the proposed city would have on the various parts of the company.

____ 3. What sources of information did you use to write the speech?

Use information on the company, the future markets, other possible locations, and positives and negatives associated with the proposed site.

____ **4.** How did you structure the information in your speech to ensure that it was organized and easy to understand, without jumping from one topic to another?
Use subheadings and paragraph titles to help break up the various subjects that are covered. Keep related materials together, making sure not to jump from one topic to another and then back again. Use an introductory statement at the beginning of the speech, and a recap at the end.

____ **5.** Who is the intended audience of the presentation, and how would their backgrounds affect the contents of the speech?
Each of the regional vice presidents has a different perspective on what would be the best location for the new plant. Be sure to address the individual needs of each.

____ **6.** From what perspective would the listeners review the speech?
Most of the vice presidents will want to be sure that each of their concerns have been commented on.

____ **7.** How familiar are the other vice presidents with the whole situation and the alternative locations?
All but one of the vice presidents are familiar with the whole situation. You should make sure that you take a little time to educate the one VP who is not, but not too much, so as not to bore the other VP's.

____ **8.** Did you avoid using superlatives, such as "absolute" and "best," to maintain impartiality?
No presentation should include superlatives. For example, you should have stated that "Riverbend has good cultural opportunities," not "incredibly terrific cultural opportunities."

___ **9.** Did you avoid using the same words or phrases over and over?
The only time to repeat exact words or phrases should be to emphasize an extremely important point. Otherwise, be sure to paraphrase previous comments.

___**10.** Did you use appropriate grammar and good paragraph construction? For example, did you make sure that each paragraph focused on only one main point and contained a topic sentence?
To maintain the flow of the speech it is important that you keep to only one concept in each paragraph. Often other points become deemphasized when they occur within the same paragraph.

___**11.** Did you use an outline format or paragraph headings to help structure the presentation?
To help break up the various major points of the speech, outlines or paragraph headings are very useful. They also help with the flow of the presentation.

___**12.** To what extent did your speech vary from the intended objectives? (In other words, did you stick to the point?)
Other points in a presentation will not be listened to, and your credibility will be lessened. Make sure only relevant material is presented in the speech.

___**13.** After you wrote the speech, did you take time to go back and reread it, to ensure that it met the general purpose of the speech and that the style and tone were appropriate for the intended audience? What style and tone did you use in the speech?
Any written document should be reviewed to ensure that the original purpose has been met and that all of the major points have been covered.

___**14.** When evaluating your speech, did you look at the total number of words, making sure you did not use too many?

Using extra words just to fill up the allotted time should be avoided. Excessive words only create confusion and cause repetitiveness and jumpiness in the presentation.

___15. When evaluating your speech, did you use appropriate vocabulary and language, making sure you avoided technical jargon and excessively long words?
It is much better to use simple, basic words to express your thoughts and ideas. Also, technical jargon will only confuse people. Avoid it as much as possible.

Write the total number of check marks here ___ .

Oral Communication

You have just completed your written report. Another aspect of effective communication has to do with oral presentations. The task you are about to begin involves the same situation, but here you will present and then critique an oral rather than written presentation.

For this task, consider the following additional circumstances:

1. Your boss was called away unexpectedly, and *you* have to make the presentation to the other regional vice presidents.
2. Tape-record your speech as if you were actually presenting it to the RVP's. As you know, the presentation is extremely important, and you need to be as clear and persuasive as possible. Treat this as if it were an actual presentation. Remember, it is supposed to last 30 minutes.

COMMUNICATOR TEST II: ORAL COMMUNICATION

To test your oral communication, you need to evaluate your speech in the following way:

1. Review the 15 questions below. They tell you what you should have done, or should have considered doing, as a benchmark against which to compare your performance. They are, however, not all-inclusive, and you, the listener, must look critically at what you have done to determine whether you have met the requirements of satisfactory performance.
2. Play back your tape-recorded speech and listen very carefully, occasionally referring to the questions.
3. Indicate with a check mark that you considered your performance on that question to be at least satisfactory.
4. Add up the check marks and write the sum on the line following the 15 questions.

____ **1.** Does your voice sound clear, and do you change your tone so that it sounds as if you are confident of your subject matter, and do you use your voice to emphasize points?

____ **2.** Do you pronounce your words clearly and not drop endings or slur them, making it difficult for your listeners to understand what you are saying?

____ **3.** Do you speak slowly enough so that each word can be heard clearly and so that the points you wish to make are emphasized?

____ **4.** Do you speak more slowly when you present some points and more rapidly for others, to help deliver your message? Avoid using a monotonous tone delivered at the same pace throughout?

____ **5.** Does the tone of your voice to provide a sincere communication?

____ **6.** Have you stated the point of your presentation in a clear fashion? (Of course it is important to present the proposed location in a favorable light.)

——— 7. Did you use nontechnical words and short sentences that emphasize points clearly?

——— 8. Does one point flow from another, and as you listen to the presentation, can you easily understand the logic of the points you are trying to make?

——— 9. Do you present some detail, but not too much, so as not to overburden your audience, with too much, for example, concerning the building of specific roads and other technical details?

———10. Is the presentation interesting? Do you present enough supporting data to back up your points, but not too much, so that your presentation becomes boring?

———11. Do you attempt any humor? Make any jokes?

———12. Do you consciously consider the variety of people who might be in the audience in your presentation?

———13. Does your tone of voice sound friendly rather than harsh?

———14. Do you hear too many "you know"'s and "see what I mean"'s and other such words extraneous to the basic message? This could include throat-clearing and the like.

———15. Do you stay on topic, consistent with your objectives?

Write the total number of check marks here ——— .

COMMUNICATOR TEST III:
FREQUENTLY MISUSED WORDS

Circle the correct meaning or usage for the words in the following list:

Word	Meaning or Usage	
1. effect	a. cause	b. influence
2. commencement	a. beginning	b. ending
3. complement	a. complete	b. praise
4. principle	a. main	b. theory
5. council	a. advice	b. group of people
6. discreet	a. distinct	b. prudent
7. following	a. subsequent	b. preceding
8. forgo	a. relinquish	b. precede
9. eminent	a. impending	b. famous
10. infer	a. assume	b. imply
11. accept	a. exclude	b. receive
12. stationary	a. fixed	b. paper
13. credible	a. remarkable	b. conceivable
14. canvass	a. cloth	b. solicit
15. devise	a. an object	b. conceive
16. alot	a. plenty	b. (not a word)
17. pretentious	a. insincere	b. sincere
18. adjunct	a. affiliate	b. competitor
19. modest	a. humble	b. confident
20. data	a. singular	b. plural

Compare your answers to the correct answers listed below. Check those you answered correctly.

____ 1. a	____ 6. b	____11. b	____16. b
____ 2. a	____ 7. a	____12. a	____17. a
____ 3. a	____ 8. a	____13. b	____18. a
____ 4. b	____ 9. b	____14. b	____19. a
____ 5. b	____10. a	____15. b	____20. b

Write the total number of check marks here ____.

COMMUNICATOR TEST IV: SPELLING

Which of the following words are spelled correctly? Place a "C" for correct or an "I" for incorrect next to each word.

_____	1. accomodate	_____	11. hurriedly
_____	2. anonymous	_____	12. interferance
_____	3. attendence	_____	13. mortgage
_____	4. bureaucracy	_____	14. maneuver
_____	5. commitee	_____	15. ommitted
_____	6. definately	_____	16. prejudice
_____	7. disipline	_____	17. reciept
_____	8. fluorescent	_____	18. restaurant
_____	9. foward	_____	19. succession
_____	10. govenor	_____	20. unamymous

Compare your answers to the correct answers listed below. Check those you answered correctly.

_____	1. I	_____	6. I	_____	11. C	_____	16. C
_____	2. C	_____	7. I	_____	12. I	_____	17. I
_____	3. I	_____	8. C	_____	13. C	_____	18. C
_____	4. C	_____	9. I	_____	14. C	_____	19. C
_____	5. I	_____	10. I	_____	15. I	_____	20. I

Write the total number of check marks here _____ .

Scoring the Communicator Tests

To score the Communicator Tests, please do the following:

1. For Test I, go back to page 123 and write down, directly below, the total number of check marks. The sum can range from 0 to 15 since there are 15 items.

    My score on Test I is _____.

2. For Test II, go back to page 128 and write down, directly below, the total number of check marks. The sum can range from 0 to 15 since there are 15 items.

    My score on Test II is _____.

3. For Test III, go back to page 130 and write down, directly below, the total number of check marks. The sum can range from 0 to 20 since there are 20 items.

    My score on Test III is _____.

4. For Test IV, go back to page 131 and write down, directly below, the total number of check marks. The sum can range from 0 to 20 since there are 20 items.

    My score on Test IV is _____.

5. Add up your scores for Tests I and II and multiply by 4. Write the sum directly below. It can range from 0 to 120.

    The sum of Tests I and II multiplied by 4 is _____.

6. Add up your scores for Tests III and IV. Write the sum directly below. It can range from 0 to 40.

    The sum of Tests III and IV is _____.

7. Add the results of steps 5 and 6, which is your total score on all four parts of the Communicator Test. It can range from 0 to 160. Write the result directly below.

My total score on Communicator Tests I through IV is _____.

Calculating and Interpreting Your Communicator mq

1. Write your score again here _____.
2. Calculate your mq by dividing your score by 160, and then multiplying by 100. Place your answer below.*

$$\frac{\text{My total score}}{160} \times 100 = \text{_____} \text{ Communicator mq.}$$

Interpretation of mq

An mq of at least 75 indicates satisfactory performance with respect to the attribute being measured. It essentially means that you earned at least 75 percent of the total possible score. This 75 percent level associated with satisfactory performance is based upon our collective experience with thousands of people taking managerial/supervisory attribute tests. As your mq approaches 100, it becomes more and more exceptional. If your mq is in the 90's, you would find yourself in approximately the top 10 percent of the test takers. With an mq in the 80's, this would place you in the top 30 percent of test takers, and an mq of 75 would mean you were in the top 50 percent of test takers. An mq of below 75 would put you in the bottom 50 percent of test takers.

Developmentally speaking, any mq of below 75 would indicate an attribute in need of development. This will be discussed in further detail in Chapter 9.

---

* Round off the result to the nearest whole number. Your mq can range from 0 to 100.

CHAPTER 6

The Meeter

The Meeter demonstrates behaviors associated with the ability to influence others and contribute to the attainment of group goals in face-to-face situations. Included in this category are the abilities to state objectives or tasks to all concerned, to inform others of what is expected of them, to direct and coordinate others in the group, and to let others know of their importance to the success of the task at hand. Additional behaviors include helping others in the group to set and clarify goals, dealing with others in the group consistent with their needs and abilities, and holding oneself responsible for the quality and quantity of work produced. The good Meeter comes into the meeting with a prepared but not inflexible agenda, evaluates and treats other group members as individuals consistent with their own goals and needs, and attempts to participate fully and set high standards of performance for the group output. The good Meeter, no matter what his or her formal authority may be, aids the group in setting and measuring objectives consistent with their resources.

In this chapter you will find a test designed to help you assess your own Meeter attribute.

THE MEETER TEST

There are a variety of situations in which the Meeter can influence others. These include four areas: meeting with subordinates, meeting with peers, meeting with customers or clients, and meeting with superiors. The following 20 multiple-choice questions, grouped according to these four areas, involve decisions concerning various situations. In answering the 20 questions, you will assume the position of Jan Brown, a sales manager for a medium-sized publishing company.

Each question poses a problem, followed by four possible solutions. Choose the one that you believe best fits the question.

Meeting with Subordinates

____ 1. You are meeting with Tom Walters, one of your sales representatives, to discuss a downward trend in his sales. During the meeting Tom becomes irritated and defensive and refuses to accept any blame for the decline. Tom claims that performance is down throughout the country, and that his performance is no worse than anyone else's. What would be the best thing to do if you wish the meeting to be as productive as possible?

    a. Ask Tom to calm down and come back and conclude the meeting when he is in a better frame of mind.

    b. Give Tom a list of what he needs to accomplish before the next meeting, which you will schedule by the end of this meeting.

    c. Present the data you have on Tom's declining performance factually without implying in any way that the issue is personal. Then begin to work with Tom on a plan for raising his sales.

    d. Inform Tom that the purpose of the meeting is to help him, not criticize him, and have him read your written review of his performance.

____ 2. You are conducting a staff meeting with a team of supervisors who report to you. During the meeting one of the newer supervisors appears distracted, like he is not listening to anything that is being said. He asks questions that have already been answered, and this is beginning to waste time. Select the statement that best expresses what you would do.

a. Ask him, "What's the matter?"

b. Ask him if he is bored with the meeting.

c. Ask him, "You seem to be concerned with something else. Would you care to discuss it after the meeting?"

d. Ignore the situation until after the meeting.

____ 3. You are about to conduct a meeting with your salespeople to discuss the large decline in sales over the past quarter. What could you do to get maximum value out of the meeting?

a. Start the presentation by comparing the performance of your district to that of the other districts. Also, be sure to compare the district to its own previous year's performance. Then explain to the salespeople what must be done if sales goals are to be met.

b. Start the presentation by comparing the performance of your district to that of the other districts. Also, be sure to compare the district to its own previous year's performance. Then ask the salespeople what they think must be done to improve sales performance.

c. Since sales performance is a sensitive subject, the best strategy would be to *not* start with a structured presentation. Instead, ask the salespeople how they feel about the sales performance of the work unit. This will allow you to ease into a conversation about poor sales.

d. Ask each sales person to present his or her own sales data along with the reasons each feels that the results are below what they should be. Out of this discussion you can identify common problem areas and let the group come up with solutions to the problems.

____ 4. You are in a meeting with your team of sales representatives, and they begin to complain that they are overworked. Committees, questionnaires from the home office, and a variety of other activities are taking them away from their main activity, that is, selling. What would you do in the meeting to begin to deal with this issue?

a. Thank them for bringing it to your attention, and tell them that you will consult with the home office and see to it that their involvement in these kinds of activities is minimized.

b. Explain to them how important these kinds of activities are and how they need to cooperate for the overall good of the organization.

c. Ask them exactly how much time is being spent on these activities. After determining and getting agreement from them on whether or not it is excessive, indicate that you will look into it further with the home office people.

d. Set up a committee of some of your better sales representatives to look into the situation with the home office personnel. Let them determine how bad the the situation really is.

_____ 5. You have been given the results of a survey, conducted by the Personnel Department, which indicate that your sales representatives find you dictatorial and difficult to deal with. You are concerned about this, but at the same time think it somewhat unfair, partially a way to excuse some of their low sales productivity. You have scheduled a meeting to discuss this. What would you say initially?

a. "It has really surprised me that you feel I'm dictatorial and difficult to deal with. I've always attempted to be understanding and get as much information as I can from all of you before I make decisions. I apologize, and I'll attempt to do better."

b. "It seems to me that the real problem with our district is not my being dictatorial, but rather the fact that I've had to push pretty hard for results recently. A lot of that has come directly from the home office and will change as soon as our figures get better. So let's start to work on how we can make that happen."

c. "Being dictatorial isn't necessarily bad. I don't have much choice on a lot of the decisions I have to make. I apologize for how you all have perceived me, and I will certainly move toward changing."

d. "I received the results of the personnel survey and was somewhat surprised that you feel I've been dictatorial and difficult to deal with. I don't want you to feel that way, so I'd like to explore with you some of the specific things I've done that have led you to feel as you do. Once we've done that, we can explore together different ways of getting done what we have to, because we do have sales productivity as a very high priority."

Meeting with Peers

____ 6. You are in a conference with managers of distribution, shipping and receiving, personnel, and maintenance to discuss the sharp incline in employee turnover. What could you do initially to make the best contribution to the meeting?

a. Suggest a better employee recruiting and orientation program.

b. Suggest a "buddy system" program as a better way of "hearing" employee problems.

c. Suggest that the Personnel Department examine the reasons for the turnover so that appropriate programs or strategies can be identified.

d. Suggest that the Personnel Department screen new employees more carefully, so that they are better qualified and therefore more likely to stay.

____ 7. You are in a meeting with the newly appointed key accounts manager and five other sales managers, attempting to work out the details of a new program. The program is designed to have major accounts receive attention from a special sales team put together to meet the customers' special needs. The team will be composed of sales representatives from the various districts. One problem is that the sales managers are concerned about losing some of their better performers to this special team. What would you suggest as a strategy for selecting the team?

a. Have each manager recommend only one person from his or her district, and suggest that the key account manager choose from among the recommendations.

b. The whole group should analyze the needs of the key accounts manager and match their recommendations to those needs, based on the strengths and weaknesses of the available salespeople. The team should then be selected by the whole group, with the approval of the new manager.

    c. Put all names of available sales representatives in a hat and have the new manager randomly choose the required number for the team. In this way, no one can protect their best performers, and it will be a fair selection system.

    d. Allow the new key accounts manager to review the records of each sales representative and make a decision. Rules could also be set up so that no one sales manager would lose more than two of his or her people. In this way, the key accounts manager will be maximally committed to her new people.

——— 8. You are meeting with a group of district managers to discuss a new sales incentive program. This team was asked to develop the new plan as a way to increase sales performance in each of the districts. Just after the meeting gets underway, the Vice President of Sales walks in and asks if she can join the meeting. As soon as she is seated, the group becomes very quiet. The conversation changes from discussing the new incentive plan to discussing superficial problems. Since everyone now seems hesitant to speak openly, what do you think you should do?

    a. Remain silent until someone else decides to say something, so you can reinforce what they say.

    b. Try to turn the conversation back to the sales incentive program by continuing to bring up suggestions, thereby demonstrating to the Vice President that her presence isn't causing any problems.

    c. Suggest that the group, now including the VP, break up into smaller subgroups to discuss the plan and then reconvene to look at all of the recommendations together.

    d. Ask the Vice President for her ideas concerning the plan.

——— 9. You are in a meeting with your peers in the Accounting Department, attempting to resolve some accounting problems. Your salespeople are not getting their commission checks in a timely manner. The Accounting Department has apparently not been following company policy and is waiting until payment is actually received from customers to issue commission checks. Their reasoning for this is that they feel that some of the salespeople are reporting sales that are not technically finalized and are unfairly receiving commission checks. What should you do?

a. State that since company policy indicates that commission checks will be issued upon receipt of a signed contract, accounting must follow that procedure.

b. Suggest that your departments jointly study information from the past six months to determine the extent to which checks have been issued prematurely. But state that in the meantime commission checks must be issued in accordance with company policy.

c. Suggest that your departments jointly study information from the past six months to determine the extent to which checks have been issued prematurely. Also, indicate that you will explain the planned study to your salespeople and will tell them that decisions will be made after the study has been completed.

d. Indicate that you will explain the problem to your salespeople and that you agree with how accounting is dealing with the problem.

___10. You are meeting with the Inventory Manager. Over the past several years there has been a recurring problem with maintaining adequate inventory during the busy summer months. Inventory has run low, and your salespeople have been forced to quote customers longer-than-usual delivery dates. This has resulted in several lost sales opportunities. You don't want the problem repeated this summer. Which of the following would be the appropriate comment to make to the Inventory Manager?

a. "We simply can't have an inventory shortage this summer. Whatever it takes, we need to ensure that we have adequate product in inventory for the summer sales goals."

b. "I understand the problems you face if you finish the summer with an inventory surplus. But a shortage of inventory puts sales in a really bad position with the customer. What can I do to help you plan the inventory needs for the summer sales months?"

c. "We have to avoid the inventory shortage we've experienced the last couple of years. I want enough inventory made up to cover the sales goals we've projected for the summer. If we don't meet the sales goals, and you end up with an inventory surplus, I'll take the full responsibility for any problems."

d. "I understand the problems you face if you finish the summer with an inventory surplus. But a shortage of inventory puts sales in a really bad position with the customer. We've provided you with a sales goal for the summer months. I'm afraid that if we have a shortage this summer, you'll have to take full responsibility for it."

Meeting with Customers or Clients

——11. You are meeting with one of your customers, who has just expressed concern over what he perceives to be a lack of follow-up service once purchases have been made. He has complained about the length of time it takes your salespeople to return his calls and their slowness in helping to resolve billing errors. At the same time, you know that this customer is exceptionally demanding and overly critical of most vendors. How would you respond to his complaint?

a. Apologize and state that you will speak to the sales staff about the problem.

b. Apologize and state that you will personally guarantee that there will be no similar problems in the future.

c. Apologize and state that you will discuss the problem with appropriate members of the sales staff and that you will contact him within a specified time to discuss specific actions to address the problem.

d. Apologize and ask what he would like you to do to avoid similar problems in the future.

——12. You and one of your sales representatives are meeting with a prospective customer whose account represents considerable long-term revenue for your company. You have discussed your proposal and the potential customer has responded positively. However, pricing is raised as an objection. The customer states that your competitor has offered essentially the same services for a slightly lower price. Your sales representative who has accompanied you on the call immediately states that your company will match the competition's pricing. What would you do?

a. Say nothing and plan to honor the sales representative's commitment.

b. Ask what price the competition has offered.

c. Indicate that some pricing adjustment could possibly be made, but that the proposed services and the competitor's pricing must be discussed further to ensure that the two proposals are equivalent.

d. Indicate that some pricing adjustment could possibly be made, but that a slightly higher pricing structure may be warranted, given the quality of the services and products offered by your company.

___13. You are making a high-level sales presentation to a group of people in a prospective customer's organization. You know only one person in the group, the contact person who originally arranged the meeting. You've been presenting for 30 minutes and still have several important points to make. You also need to cover the entire pricing portion of your proposal. One of the group members, whom you do not know, interrupts and asks that you conclude your presentation. In doing this, he indicates that the 30 minutes that had been allocated for your presentation is up, and the group has other topics to discuss. You are positive your contact person told you explicitly that you would have up to one hour for your presentation. What would your first response be?

a. Explain that you thought more time had been allocated for the presentation, and then ask for five more minutes to summarize the major points that have not been covered.

b. Turn to your contact person and explain that you were under the impression that one hour had been allocated for the presentation.

c. Explain that you were under the impression that one hour had been allocated for the presentation, and indicate that you would like the opportunity to complete your presentation.

d. Explain that you thought more time had been allocated for the presentation, and indicate that the written proposal you will leave with the group covers the points you have been unable to present orally.

___**14.** You are meeting with a customer and have been answering her questions regarding a sales contract you sent her last week. You feel that all of the issues have been addressed, and are about to suggest that she sign the contract if she has no more questions. Suddenly her boss comes in and asks her to join him for lunch. He states that he needs to discuss some issues with her before he leaves on a business trip. You know her boss only casually. What should you do?
  a. Suggest that since all of the questions appear to have been covered, she should sign the contract now.
  b. Ask her if she would like you to join them for lunch in order to finish the discussion.
  c. Ask her what time she would like to meet to finish the discussion.
  d. Suggest to her a specific time for resuming your meeting.

___**15.** Your contact at an organization you've been trying to present to for some time has called and informed you that tomorrow you can present to a management steering committee. However, only 30 minutes will be available. You feel you need at least an hour for an adequate presentation of the benefits of your product. Your contact has also indicated that if you cannot make the presentation tomorrow, it may be a month or more before another meeting date could be scheduled. What should you do?
  a. Indicate that it would be better to postpone the presentation until a later date when more time would be available.
  b. Plan to do the presentation tomorrow and, once in the meeting, attempt to gain additional time from the group members.
  c. Plan to do the presentation tomorrow, highlighting major points as well as possible, and, at the conclusion of the meeting, attempt to gain a commitment for a second meeting.
  d. Plan to do the presentation tomorrow, highlighting major points as well as possible, and augment your oral presentation with pertinent written materials provided to each member of the group.

Meeting with Superiors

___16. During a meeting your boss indicates that she is disappointed with your group's sales results this past quarter on a newly introduced product. Your group is currently at 80 percent of quota on the new product. She asks for your input on improving the situation. What should you do?

    a. State that you'll meet with the sales representatives and tell them to put more emphasis on the new product.

    b. State that you'll meet regularly with each sales representative to monitor and discuss sales of the new product.

    c. Acknowledge the problem and ask her for suggestions.

    d. State that you'll put together a plan and will discuss it with her next week.

___17. During your performance appraisal, your boss briefly states that your performance has been "well above satisfactory" (the next to the highest performance rating you could receive). She adds that it will result in a significant merit pay increase for you. This is essentially the extent of her comments, and she appears ready to end the meeting. What should you do?

    a. Thank her, but cite your positive accomplishments for the year and explain why you feel you should be rated slightly higher.

    b. Thank her and allow the meeting to end.

    c. Ask her to discuss the specific areas where improvement would be most warranted.

    d. Ask her to discuss the general areas in which your performance was viewed as being strongest.

___18. You are in a meeting with your boss and your boss' boss. During the meeting your boss presents some information that you know is incorrect. What do you think should be done?

    a. Say nothing until after the meeting.

    b. Tell your boss that you think that the information is incorrect.

    c. Ask your boss if she meant to say that.

d. Tell your boss's boss that the information has been recently changed and then present the correct information.

___19. You have been asked to design a task force to help determine the new compensation schedule for all clericals within the company. What is the major issue to consider in structuring the group?

a. Create a group that will allow high-level managers to make the decisions.

b. Create a group that will be made up of all levels of the organization, so that both high-level and lower-level personnel can be involved in the decisions.

c. Break into smaller groups composed of personnel at the same level and collect their inputs separately.

d. Create a group of lower-level personnel, since they are closer to the clericals in terms of organizational level.

___20. An opportunity has come up for you to take a job with another company. In your mind, there are many more long-term career opportunities with the new company. You have been quite happy in your current job, and you don't want to leave before discussing the situation with your boss. How would you begin the meeting with your boss?

a. "I need to let you know that I've been offered a job that I'm thinking of taking, but before I make my final decision, I'd like to see what my career opportunities are here."

b. "I've been wondering about my long-term career opportunities with the company. I like it here and I just want to make sure that I will have the opportunity to grow."

c. "I like working here but I have some concerns with my future opportunities."

d. Tell your boss that you've been offered another job, which you will take unless she can promise you similar opportunities with the company.

Scoring the Meeter Test

On the following pages are the correct answers to the multiple-choice questions. Accompanying each correct answer is a short explanation.

1. Compare your choice to the correct answer on all 20 questions. Place a check mark by each question you answered correctly. Be sure to read the explanation for the correct choice for each question.
2. Add up the check marks. The sum can range from 0 to 20.
3. Write the sum in the space below.

My score on the Meeter Test is _____ .

Correct Answers and Explanations

Q#	ANS	Explanation
____ 1.	c.	Begin immediately to work on the problem. In addition, begin to work on a performance improvement plan. Avoiding by rescheduling, delivering a list of goals, or assuring him that you are interested in working with him rather than criticizing him, along with having him read your written review of him, are not as effective.
____ 2.	d.	Most important, never embarrass anyone in front of others. The situation, although annoying and distracting, should be dealt with at a later time. Acknowledging his having something on his mind and scheduling a discussion after the meeting is not as bad a choice as the two remaining ones, but it is still drawing attention to him in the presence of others.
____ 3.	b.	Immediately position the meeting by pointing out the facts. Then use the meeting to explore with the group means by which sales goals can be reached. By including the group in possible solutions you will have

better acceptance of whatever is implemented to solve the problem. This is a preferable strategy to simply telling them what must be done, or not structuring the meeting and running the risk of not coming up with solutions, or simply comparing the results of the sales representatives, thereby possibly singling out poor performers in front of the group.

_____ 4. c. You cannot promise minimal involvement for them without collecting further information, nor should you simply back the position that they need to do those things because of their importance to the company. The setting up of a committee with home office personnel would likely be cumbersome at this point, without first exploring the issues with them.

_____ 5. d. The first thing you need to do is gather more information. You cannot minimize the productivity issue, but before changing your behavior you need to look further into the issue. However, you do not want to imply that your behavior is all because of the push for productivity.

_____ 6. c. The reasons for turnover must be ascertained first. After this is done, better hiring, a "buddy system," or better employee recruiting and orientation programs might make sense.

_____ 7. b. The best way to work out this problem is logically, not politically. The needs of the new team as well as the needs of the existing districts must be taken into account. Trading people, or having managers simply recommend whomever they want from their districts without a uniform concern for what must be accomplished is not in the best interest of the company. Simply allowing the new sales manager to select from among all other districts could develop an overall weakening of some of the other districts. Moreover, since she is new, she might not use some valuable information about the sales representatives that would otherwise come out in a discussion with all the managers; and randomly selecting people rarely works as a best solution.

_____ 8. c. Dividing into smaller groups will ensure more input, because only one of the groups will be directly affected by the presence of the VP. Therefore, in all of the other groups, the conversation will turn back to the task at hand. Inviting the VP to state her ideas may greatly affect the thinking and actions of the group members, while remaining silent until someone else speaks, or "talking too much," will not necessarily have the desired effect of really getting the group to accomplish the task.

_____ 9. b. Accounting has provided no evidence to support the fact that a problem actually exists. Thus, a study to determine the extent of the problem is needed. However, should a problem exist, there are other alternatives for dealing with it. Timely payment of the salespeople, per company policy, is important for maintaining motivation and performance of the sales staff.

_____10. b. Joint problem solving will produce the best results for the organization as a whole. Threats and finger-pointing are unproductive. Also, who will be held accountable for the problem should it occur is unimportant. If either a surplus or a shortage of inventory occurs, the whole company suffers.

_____11. b. Vague assurances are unlikely to satisfy the customer. Asking the customer for suggestions on such simple issues may result in unrealistic demands being made. Further investigation of the matter and the promise of a specific plan being delivered within a specified time will demonstrate concern and commitment to the customer.

____12. c. Some verbal response is required. It is critical to determine the truth of the customer's statement, that a competitor has offered similar services at a lower price structure, while at the same time displaying at least a willingness to consider a price reduction. Knocking the competition may be viewed as unprofessional by the customer.

____13. a. Drawing your contact person into the discussion at this point will serve no useful purpose. Likewise, to ask for an additional 30 minutes displays a total disregard for the priorities of the group. The written proposal can be left with the group under any circumstances. Asking for five more minutes displays a responsiveness to the needs of the group and also allows you to at least highlight the key points you want the group to remember.

____14. a. Push for the close now. Delaying the signing could only have negative consequences. Inviting yourself for lunch would be inappropriate and only delays the close.

____15. c. Get to the group now. Use this first meeting to generate interest and support. Details can be covered in a second meeting if in the initial meeting the group shows interest. Asking for more time once you are in the meeting may cause resentment on the part of your contact person. Written materials are always appreciated, but should not serve as a substitute for personal contact.

____16. d. Vague assurances and courses of action are unlikely to satisfy her. Asking for her input before you have investigated potential causes of the problem serves no purpose. Take responsibility for looking into the problem and set a specific follow-up time for discussing your suggestions.

____17. c. Seeking specific feedback on your performance will provide the greatest opportunity for development and improvement. Also, actively demonstrating a desire to learn and improve is highly valued by superiors.

_____18. a. You should rarely if ever correct your boss in front of their boss. Speaking directly to your boss's boss makes it look like your boss is not on top of all of the information regarding the meeting, and questioning your boss may create doubts during the meeting.

_____19. b. When policies are being developed that will affect many different levels in an organization, all affected levels should be included in the decision-making process when possible. This allows for more agreement among those included.

_____20. b. You shouldn't be confrontational with your boss. Simply asking about your future with the company and not mentioning the possible new job meets all of your needs without jeopardizing your future.

Calculating and Interpreting Your Meeter mq

1. Write your score again here _____ .
2. Calculate your mq by dividing your score by 20, and then multiplying by 100. Place your answer directly below.*

$$\frac{\text{My total score}}{20} \times 100 = \underline{\hspace{1.5cm}} \text{ Meeter mq.}$$

Interpretation of mq

An mq of at least 75 indicates satisfactory performance with respect to the attribute being measured. It essentially means that you earned

---

* Round off the result to the nearest whole number. Your mq can range from 0 to 100.

at least 75 percent of the total possible score. This 75 percent level associated with satisfactory performance is based upon our collective experience with thousands of people taking managerial/supervisory attribute tests. As your mq approaches 100, it becomes more and more exceptional. If your mq is in the 90's, you would find yourself in approximately the top 10 percent of the test takers. With an mq in the 80's, this would place you in the top 30 percent of test takers, and an mq of 75 would mean you were in the top 50 percent of test takers. An mq of below 75 would put you in the bottom 50 percent of test takers.

Developmentally speaking, any mq of below 75 would indicate an attribute in need of development. This will be discussed in further detail in Chapter 9.

CHAPTER 7

The Mentor

The Mentor demonstrates behaviors associated with developing and nurturing other individuals in order to allow them to grow to their maximum level of effectiveness in a given situation. Included in this attribute are the following abilities: evaluating other individuals' strengths and weaknesses, a willingness to work with them and offer them opportunities to try things, and providing feedback on the quality of their attempts. In addition, the good Mentor, like the good coach, gives feedback continuously, not only on results, but also on how people are accomplishing their tasks, and continuously searches for learning situations and opportunities that will allow them to grow. In other words, the Mentor develops another by establishing a close and trusting relationship, thereby establishing an environment in which the individual feels comfortable making decisions and taking risks. On the following pages you will find a test designed to help you assess your own Mentor attribute.

THE MENTOR TEST

The questionnaire that follows contains a series of 35 statements. Each statement represents a belief you hold or a behavior you practice, or *would practice if given the opportunity*. In this test you will indicate the extent to which you agree or disagree with each statement.

Refer to the rating scale below. Place the number that indicates the extent of your agreement or disagreement with a particular statement alongside that statement. Please respond to all 35 statements.

Bear in mind that when we are asked to answer questions about ourselves it is sometimes difficult to interpret how we *really* feel about something. In this test we want you to attempt to go beyond your own feelings about yourself, by following these three steps:

1. Before you begin the test, select three to five people to whom you are or were a mentor, either formally or informally. If you are not now a manager or a supervisor, you may consider other situations in which you were a mentor, for example, to a fellow worker, or as a coach, or perceived as such in school, or when interacting with children or other family members, or in church or with civic groups. If you are or have ever been a supervisor or manager, certainly you are or were a mentor to your subordinates.
2. As you look at each statement, think about what each of those people you identified would say about you if they were asked to rate you on the same 7-point scale.
3. In rating the statements, base your ratings not only on *your perception* of yourself or the level of belief you hold or the behaviors you practice, but also on a composite of how you believe those three to five people would rate you on the extent to which you actually demonstrated the behavior associated with each statement.

Mentor Rating Scale

Rating	Category
7	Very strongly agree
6	Strongly agree
5	Agree
4	Slightly agree to slightly disagree
3	Disagree
2	Strongly disagree
1	Very strongly disagree

____ 1. I think it's important to help others grow.

____ 2. I think it's important to be honest with people; to point out areas that need improvement as well as their strengths.

____ 3. I think it's important to give feedback frequently; this will encourage learning.

____ 4. When giving feedback, it's critical to be as specific as possible.

____ 5. One of the key elements in working with other people is establishing trust.

____ 6. Within reason, it is desirable to encourage other people to take risks.

____ 7. I think it's important to have subordinates to dinner on occasion, or to go out to lunch with them.

____ 8. I like others to see me as a person to talk to, to discuss their problems with, or to confide in.

____ 9. I think it's important to identify ways people can improve themselves.

____10. It's important to communicate to others the expectations of the organization, for example, the dress code, what really counts, and so on.

____11. To help others succeed in the organization, it's important to let them know who the "really powerful" people are.

____12. I think it's important to create a nonthreatening environment in which ideas and feelings may be safely expressed.

___13. It's important to help others develop technical skills as well as managerial skills.

___14. I wouldn't hesitate to let my subordinates sit in on a top-level meeting where I am present so they could observe and learn.

___15. I think it's important to go to bat for your subordinates if they have not been dealt with fairly.

___16. I wouldn't be reluctant to transfer one of my most valued subordinates if it was in his or her best interests, developmentally speaking.

___17. I wouldn't be reluctant to sponsor one of my valued subordinates for a special assignment if it was in his or her best interests, developmentally speaking.

___18. I think it's important to protect my subordinates from high-risk situations, for example, loss of job.

___19. I would go out of my way to open doors for someone who I thought was deserving.

___20. I would try to bypass red tape to help someone who I thought was deserving.

___21. It's important to recognize and support another's dreams.

___22. It's desirable, at the appropriate time, to create situations that allow others to become more visible or that increase their exposure in the organization.

___23. It's important to encourage the independence of others.

___24. I think it's critical to allow highly valued subordinates to be promoted, even though it might detract from my own functional area.

___25. It's desirable to make sure people are in challenging positions.

___26. It's important to be seen as a person who is able to tell others whether or not their goals are realistic.

___27. I think it's important to be seen as a role model for others.

___28. I think it's important to give others the chance to make mistakes.

___29. I enjoy working with younger or less-experienced people in order to help them learn.

___30. I feel good if someone I've helped progresses in the organization.

___31. It doesn't bother me if someone I've helped actually moves ahead of me in the organization.

___32. I think you gain power in the eyes of key people in the organization if people you've helped grow advance in the organization.

___33. It's important to allow others to come up with creative solutions to problems.

___34. It's important to stimulate the ideas of others.

___35. It's important to confront and challenge your subordinates.

Scoring the Mentor Test

1. Add up the ratings. The sum can range from 35 to 245.
2. Write the sum in the space below.

My score on the Mentor Test is _____ .

Calculating and Interpreting Your Mentor mq

1. Write your score again here _____ .
2. Calculate your mq by dividing your score by 245, and then multiplying by 100. Place your answer directly below.*

$$\frac{\text{My total score}}{245} \times 100 = \underline{\hspace{2cm}} \text{ Mentor mq.}$$

Interpretation of mq

An mq of at least 75 indicates satisfactory performance with respect to the attribute being measured. It essentially means that you earned at least 75 percent of the total possible score. This 75 percent level associated with satisfactory performance is based upon our collective experience with thousands of people taking managerial/supervisory attribute tests. As your mq approaches 100, it becomes more and more exceptional. If your mq is in the 90's, you would find yourself in approximately the top 10 percent of the test takers. With an mq in the 80's, this would place you in the top 30 percent of test takers, and an

_____

* Round off the result to the nearest whole number. Your mq can range from 0 to 100.

mq of 75 would mean you were in the top 50 percent of test takers. An mq of below 75 would put you in the bottom 50 percent of test takers.

Developmentally speaking, any mq of below 75 would indicate an attribute in need of development. This will be discussed in further detail in Chapter 9.

CHAPTER 8

The Aspirer

The Aspirer demonstrates behaviors associated with striving for a goal. The Aspirer constantly looks toward the future and works toward a greater level of perfection, a higher position, or, generally, a better position on the job or in life. The Aspirer is characterized by a great need for achievement, a willingness to work hard, and a constant focus on a goal. In addition, Aspirers gain pleasure from their achievements and, no matter the environment in which they find themselves, will continuously ask questions, search for alternative answers, and try to better their position. Aspirers will "aspire" toward perfection in managerial/supervisory situations because their values and goals are consistent with those associated with the managerial/supervisory situations.

On the following pages you will find a test designed to help you assess your own Aspirer attribute.

Instructions and Test Information

In this chapter we measure the extent to which you confront (or would confront) challenges that require considerable effort and that are stress inducing, often associated with people conflicts. These are basic managerial/supervisory challenges.

Following are 13 brief statements, each one pertaining to a specific job activity. Read each of these statements carefully. In the Aspirer Test you will be presented with pairs of these statements. For each pair, you are asked to choose which you would *prefer* to do. There are 40 pairs. Choose one statement for each pair.

The Aspirer Test is a measure of your preferences, not a test of your competencies. Your responses should reflect your true feelings.

1. You have been assigned a new project and a given deadline for completing it. You will be solely responsible for determining the different activities that need to be done, the order in which they will need to be done, and so on.

2. You have been elected to represent your department on a special committee made up of individuals from different departments within the company. The purpose of the committee is to discuss and resolve several problems that are impacting your department and the other departments represented on the committee. You will have to present your views and opinions in a clear and forceful manner, defend them to the other committee members, and ultimately negotiate solutions with the other committee members.

3. You have been asked by your manager to conduct a day-long training session with several newer employees in the work unit. The session involves explaining the company's employee benefits program. Conducting the session will require you to make several formal presentations to the group and facilitate several group discussion sessions with the employees.

4. You have been given the responsibility for evaluating a new piece of equipment that the work unit is considering purchasing. The equipment could significantly improve the overall productivity of the unit. You will need to assess current productivity, assess the potential impact of the new equipment, evaluate the cost of the proposed equipment relative to potential productivity increases, etc. and submit a recommendation to your manager.

5. You have been assigned to handle a somewhat complicated project that the unit unexpectedly received. The project has a tight deadline, and you have been put in charge of two other staff members who will assist you with the project. You will be responsible for

developing all timetables for the project, including detailed schedules for yourself and the two other staff members assigned to the project.

6. You are responsible for training a new employee in the work unit. You will be responsible for reviewing her work, providing feedback to her regarding work she submits, and evaluating her general performance after she has been in the unit for two months.

7. Two employees in the unit have had several significant arguments over the past two months, and there is considerable tension between them. One of the two employees comes to you and asks you to meet with the two of them to see if you can help mediate the situation.

8. One of your employees, who reports directly to you, has been late in completing the last several assignments you gave him. This has created problems for the work unit. You must meet with the employee and tell him that this situation can no longer continue and that he must submit his assignments in a more timely manner.

9. You have been asked to develop a standardized procedure for the manner in which technical proposals are prepared. Once developed, the standards will be used by everyone in the work unit.

10. During the past month you have been studing different companies that could provide raw materials and supplies to your organization. There are three companies that could be selected. You need to determine which of the three you will select as your supplier and present your recommendation and supporting rational to your immediate manager, as well as to his boss.

11. You have been given the opportunity to attend a three-month training course that will enhance your technical skills. After attending the session, you will be solely responsible for doing the portions of any projects the work unit undertakes that involve this particular technology.

12. Your manager has asked that, for the next month, you work closely with a relatively new employee in the work unit. Thus far the employee has demonstrated less than adequate job performance. At the end of the month the employee will finish her probationary

employment period, and your manager will want you to make a recommendation as to whether the employee should be retained or terminated.

13. You have an opportunity to take full responsibility for personally doing all sales presentations required of the work unit.

THE ASPIRER TEST

Following are the 13 job activity statements you have just read, now arranged in 40 pairs. You need to indicate for each pair which activity you would prefer to do by placing a check mark beside that statement. *Check only one statement for each pair,* even if you feel that neither activity is something you would really prefer to do.

1.

12. Your manager has asked that, for the next month, you work closely with a relatively new employee in the work unit. Thus far the employee has demonstrated less than adequate job performance. At the end of the month the employee will finish her probationary employment period, and your manager will want you to make a recommendation as to whether the employee should be retained or terminated.

or

9. You have been asked to develop a standardized procedure for the manner in which technical proposals are prepared. Once developed, the standards will be used by everyone in the work unit.

2.   4. You have been given the re- *or* 3. You have been asked by your
sponsibility for evaluating a new   manager to conduct a day-long
piece of equipment that the work   training session with several
unit is considering purchasing.   newer employees in the work
The equipment could signifi-   unit. The session involves ex-
cantly improve the overall pro-   plaining the company's employee
ductivity of the unit. You will   benefits program. Conducting
need to assess current productiv-   the session will require you to
ity, assess the potential impact of   make several formal presenta-
the new equipment, evaluate the   tions to the group and facilitate
cost of the proposed equipment   several group discussion sessions
relative to potential productivity   with the employees.
increases, etc. and submit a rec-
ommendation to your manager.

3.   1. You have been assigned a new *or* 2. You have been elected to rep-
project and given a deadline for   resent your department on a spe-
completing it. You will be solely   cial committee made up of
responsible for determining the   individuals from different de-
different activities that need to be   partments within the company.
done, the order in which they   The purpose of the committee is
will need to be done, and so on.   to discuss and resolve several
                                         problems that are impacting
                                         your department and the other
                                         departments represented on the
                                         committee. You will have to
                                         present your views and opinions
                                         in a clear and forceful manner,
                                         defend them to the other com-
                                         mittee members, and ultimately
                                         negotiate solutions with the
                                         other committee members.

4.

11. You have been given the opportunity to attend a three-month training course that will enhance your technical skills. After attending the session, you will be solely responsible for doing the portions of any projects the work unit undertakes that involve this particular technology.

or

2. You have been elected to represent your department on a special committee made up of individuals from different departments within the company. The purpose of the committee is to discuss and resolve several problems that are impacting your departments and the other departments represented on the committee. You will have to present your views and opinions in a clear and forceful manner, defend them to the other committee members, and ultimately negotiate solutions with the other committee members.

5.

3. You have been asked by your manager to conduct a day-long training session with several newer employees in the work unit. The session involves explaining the company's employee benefits program. Conducting the session will require you to make several formal presentations to the group and facilitate several group discussion sessions with the employees.

or

1. You have been assigned a new project and a deadline for completing it. You will be solely responsible for determining the different activities that need to be done, the order in which they will need to be done, and so on.

6.

2. You have been elected to represent your department on a special committee made up of individuals from different departments within the company. The purpose of the committee is to discuss and resolve several problems that are impacting your department and the other departments represented on the committee. You will have to present your views and opinions in a clear and forceful manner, defend them to the other committee members, and ultimately negotiate solutions with the other committee members.

or 9. You have been asked to develop a standardized procedure for the manner in which technical proposals are prepared. Once developed, the standards will be used by everyone in the work unit.

7.

11. You have been given the opportunity to attend a three-month training course that will enhance your technical skills. After attending the session, you will be solely responsible for doing the portions of any projects the work unit undertakes that involve this particular technology.

or 5. You have been assigned to handle a somewhat complicated project that the unit unexpectedly received. The project has a tight deadline, and you have been put in charge of two other staff members who will assist you with the project. You will be responsible for developing all timetables for the project, including detailed schedules for yourself and the two other staff members assigned to the project.

8.

9. You have been asked to develop a standardized procedure for the manner in which technical proposals are prepared. Once developed, the standards will be used by everyone in the work unit.

or 10. During the past month, you have been studying different companies that could provide raw materials and supplies to your organization. There are three companies that could be selected. You need to determine which of the three you will select as your supplier and present your recommendation and supporting rational to your immediate manager, as well as to his boss.

9.

1. You have been assigned a new project and a deadline for completing it. You will be solely responsible for determining the different activities that need to be done, the order in which they will need to be done, and so on.

or 12. Your manager has asked that, for the next month, you work closely with a relatively new employee in the work unit. Thus far the employee has demonstrated less than adequate job performance. At the end of the month the employee will finish her probationary employment period, and your manager will want you to make a recommendation as to whether the employee should be retained or terminated.

10.   13. You have an opportunity to *or* 2. You have been elected to represent your department on a special committee made up of individuals from different departments within the company. The purpose of the committee is to discuss and resolve several problems that are impacting your department and the other departments represented on the committee. You will have to present your views and opinions in a clear and forceful manner, defend them to the other committee members, and ultimately negotiate solutions with the other committee members.

11.   5. You have been assigned to *or* 4. You have been given the responsibility for evaluating a new piece of equipment that the work unit is considering purchasing. The equipment could significantly improve the overall productivity of the unit. You will need to assess current productivity, assess the potential impact of the new equipment, evaluate the cost of the proposed equipment relative to potential productivity increases, and submit a recommendation to your manager.

12.   13. You have an opportunity to *or* 5. You have been assigned to
take full responsibility for per- handle a somewhat complicated
sonally doing all sales presenta- project that the unit unexpect-
tions required of the work unit. edly received. The project has a
tight deadline, and you have
been put in charge of two other
staff members who will assist
you with the project. You will be
responsible for developing all
timetables for the project, including detailed schedules for yourself and the two other staff
members assigned to the project.

13.   7. Two employees in the unit *or* 13. You have an opportunity to
have had several significant ar- take full responsibility for per-
guments over the past two sonally doing all sales presenta-
months, and there is consider- tions required of the work unit.
able tension between them. One
of the two employees comes to
you and asks you to meet with
the two of them to see if you can
help mediate the situation.

14.   10. During the past month you *or* 1. You have been assigned a new
have been studying different project and given a deadline for
companies that could provide completing it. You will be solely
raw materials and supplies to responsible for determining the
your organization. There are different activities that need to be
three companies that could be se- done, the order in which they
lected. You need to determine will need to be done, and so on.
which of the three you will select
as your supplier and present your
recommendation and supporting
rational to your immediate manager, as well as to his boss.

15.   10. During the past month you *or* 13. You have an opportunity to have been studying different take full responsibility for per- companies that could provide sonally doing all sales presenta- raw materials and supplies to tions required of the work unit. your organization. There are three companies that could be se- lected. You need to determine which of the three you will select as your supplier and present your recommendation and supporting rational to your immediate man- ager, as well as to his boss.

16.   5. You have been assigned to *or* 1. You have been assigned a new handle a somewhat complicated project and given a deadline for project that the unit unexpect- completing it. You will be solely edly received. The project has a responsible for determining the tight deadline, and you have different activities that need to be been put in charge of two other done, the order in which they staff members who will assist will need to be done, and so on. you with the project. You will be responsible for developing all timetables for the project, includ- ing detailed schedules for your- self and the two other staff members assigned to the project.

17. 7. Two employees in the unit *or* have had several significant arguments over the past two months, and there is considerable tension between them. One of the two employees comes to you and asks you to meet with the two of them to see if you can help mediate the situation.

11. You have been given the opportunity to attend a three-month training course that will enhance your technical skills. After attending the session, you will be solely responsible for doing the portions of any projects the work unit undertakes that involve this particular technology.

18. 6. You are responsible for training a new employee in the work *or* unit. You will be responsible for reviewing her work, providing feedback to her regarding work she submits, and evaluating her general performance after she has been in the unit for two months.

4. You have been given the responsibility for evaluating a new piece of equipment that the work unit is considering purchasing. The equipment could significantly improve the overall productivity of the unit. You will need to assess current productivity, assess the potential impact of the new equipment, evaluate the cost of the proposed equipment relative to potential productivity increases, and submit a recommendation to your manager.

19.   8. One of your employees, who *or* 13. You have an opportunity to take full responsibility for personally doing all sales presentations required of the work unit.

reports directly to you, has been late in completing the last several assignments you gave him. This has created problems for the work unit. You must meet with the employee and tell him that this situation can no longer continue and that he must submit his assignments in a more timely manner.

20.   9. You have been asked to develop a standardized procedure for the manner in which technical proposals are prepared. Once developed, the standards will be used by everyone in the work unit. *or* 8. One of your employees, who reports directly to you, has been late in completing the last several assignments you gave him. This has created problems for the work unit. You must meet with the employee and tell him that this situation can no longer continue and that he must submit his assignments in a more timely manner.

21.   12. Your manager has asked *or* that, for the next month, you work closely with a relatively new employee in the work unit. Thus far the employee has demonstrated less than adequate job performance. At the end of the month the employee will finish her probationary employment period, and your manager will want you to make a recommendation as to whether the employee should be retained or terminated.

13. You have an opportunity to take full responsibility for personally doing all sales presentations required of the work unit.

22.   6. You are responsible for training a new employee in the work unit. You will be responsible for reviewing her work, providing feedback to her regarding work she submits, and evaluating her general performance after she has been in the unit for two months. *or*

11. You have been given the opportunity to attend a three-month training course that will enhance your technical skills. After attending the session, you will be solely responsible for doing the portions of any projects the work unit undertakes that involve this particular technology.

23.   3. You have been asked by your *or* 13. You have an opportunity to take full responsibility for personally doing all sales presentations required of the work unit.

manager to conduct a day-long training session with several newer employees in the work unit. The session involves explaining the company's employee benefits program. Conducting the session will require you to make several formal presentations to the group and facilitate several group discussion sessions with the employees.

24.   4. You have been given the re- *or* 7. Two employees in the unit have had several significant arguments over the past two months, and there is considerable tension between them. One of the two employees comes to you and asks you to meet with the two of them to see if you can help mediate the situation.

sponsibility for evaluating a new piece of equipment that the work unit is considering purchasing. The equipment could significantly improve the overall productivity of the unit. You will need to assess current productivity, assess the potential impact of the new equipment, evaluate the cost of the proposed equipment relative to potential productivity increases, and submit a recommendation to your manager.

25.   1. You have been assigned a new *or* 6. You are responsible for training a new employee in the work project and given a deadline for unit. You will be responsible for completing it. You will be solely reviewing her work, providing responsible for determining the feedback to her regarding work different activities that need to be she submits, and evaluating her done, the order in which they general performance after she will need to be done, and so on. has been in the unit for two months.

26.   5. You have been assigned to *or* 9. You have been asked to develop handle a somewhat complicated a standardized procedure for the project that the unit unexpect- manner in which technical pro- edly received. The project has a posals are prepared. Once devel- tight deadline, and you have oped, the standards will be used been put in charge of two other by everyone in the work unit. staff members who will assist you with the project. You will be responsible for developing all timetables for the project, includ- ing detailed schedules for your- self and the two other staff members assigned to the project.

27.   9. You have been asked to de- *or* 7. Two employees in the unit velop a standardized procedure have had several significant ar- for the manner in which techni- guments over the past two cal proposals are prepared. Once months, and there is consider- developed, the standards will be able tension between them. One used by everyone in the work of the two employees comes to unit. you and asks you to meet with the two of them to see if you can help mediate the situation.

28. 7. Two employees in the unit *or* 1. You have been assigned a new
have had several significant ar-
guments over the past two
months, and there is considerable tension between them. One
of the two employees comes to
you and asks you to meet with
the two of them to see if you can
help mediate the situation.

project and given a deadline for
completing it. You will be solely
responsible for determining the
different activities that need to be
done, the order in which they
will need to be done, and so on.

29. 12. Your manager has asked *or* 4. You have been given the re-
that, for the next month, you
work closely with a relatively
new employee in the work unit.
Thus far the employee has demonstrated less than adequate job
performance. At the end of the
month the employee will finish
her probationary employment
period, and your manager will
want you to make a recommendation as to whether the employee should be retained or
terminated.

sponsibility for evaluating a new
piece of equipment that the work
unit is considering purchasing.
The equipment could significantly improve the overall productivity of the unit. You will
need to assess current productivity, assess the potential impact of
the new equipment, evaluate the
cost of the proposed equipment
relative to potential productivity
increases, and submit a recommendation to your manager.

30. 10. During the past month you *or* 11. You have been given the opportunity to attend a three-month training course that will enhance your technical skills. After attending the session, you will be solely responsible for doing the portions of any projects the work unit undertakes that involve this particular technology.

have been studying different companies that could provide raw materials and supplies to your organization. There are three companies that could be selected. You need to determine which of the three you will select as your supplier and present your recommendation and supporting rational to your immediate manager, as well as to his boss.

31. 8. One of your employees, who *or* 1. You have been assigned a new project and given a deadline for completing it. You will be solely responsible for determining the different activities that need to be done, the order in which they will need to be done, and so on.

reports directly to you, has been late in completing the last several assignments you gave him. This has created problems for the work unit. You must meet with the employee and tell him that this situation can no longer continue and that he must submit his assignments in a more timely manner.

32.   11. You have been given the op- *or* 12. Your manager has asked
portunity to attend a three-month training course that will enhance your technical skills. After attending the session, you will be solely responsible for doing the portions of any projects the work unit undertakes that involves this particular technology.

that, for the next month, you work closely with a relatively new employee in the work unit. Thus far the employee has demonstrated less than adequate job performance. At the end of the month the employee will finish her probationary employment period, and your manager will want you to make a recommendation as to whether the employee should be retained or terminated.

33.   8. One of your employees, who *or* 4. You have been given the re-
reports directly to you, has been late in completing the last several assignments you gave him. This has created problems for the work unit. You must meet with the employee and tell him that this situation can no longer continue and that he must submit his assignments in a more timely manner.

sponsibility for evaluating a new piece of equipment that the work unit is considering purchasing. The equipment could significantly improve the overall productivity of the unit. You will need to assess current productivity, assess the potential impact of the new equipment, evaluate the cost of the proposed equipment relative to potential productivity increases, and submit a recommendation to your manager.

34. 3. You have been asked by your *or* 9. You have been asked to de-
manager to conduct a day-long velop a standardized procedure
training session with several for the manner in which techni-
newer employees in the work cal proposals are prepared. Once
unit. The session involves ex- developed, the standards will be
plaining the company's employee used by everyone in the work
benefits program. Conducting unit.
the session will require you to
make several formal presentations to the group and facilitate
several group discussion sessions
with the employees.

35. 13. You have an opportunity to *or* 6. You are responsible for train-
take full responsibility for per- ing a new employee in the work
sonally doing all sales presenta- unit. You will be responsible for
tions required of the work unit. reviewing her work, providing
feedback to her regarding work
she submits, and evaluating her
general performance after she
has been in the unit for two
months.

36. 6. You are responsible for train- *or* 9. You have been asked to de-
ing a new employee in the work velop a standardized procedure
unit. You will be responsible for for the manner in which techni-
reviewing her work, providing cal proposals are prepared. Once
feedback to her regarding work developed, the standards will be
she submits, and evaluating her used by everyone in the work
general performance after she unit.
has been in the unit for two
months.

37.   3. You have been asked by your *or* 11. You have been given the opportunity to attend a three month training course that will enhance your technical skills. After attending the session, you will be solely responsible for doing the portions of any projects the work unit undertakes that involve this particular technology.

manager to conduct a day-long training session with several newer employees in the work unit. The session involves explaining the company's employee benefits program. Conducting the session will require you to make several formal presentations to the group and facilitate several group discussion sessions with the employees.

38.   11. You have been given the opportunity to attend a three-month training course that will enhance your technical skills. After attending the session, you will be solely responsible for doing the portions of any projects the work unit undertakes that involve this particular technology. *or* 8. One of your employees, who reports directly to you, has been late in completing the last several assignments you gave him. This has created problems for the work unit. You must meet with the employee and tell him that this situation can no longer continue and that he must submit his assignments in a more timely manner.

39. 4. You have been given the responsibility for evaluating a new piece of equipment that the work unit is considering purchasing. The equipment could significantly improve the overall productivity of the unit. You will need to assess current productivity, assess the potential impact of the new equipment, evaluate the cost of the proposed equipment relative to potential productivity increases, and submit a recommendation to your manager.

or 10. During the past month you have been studying different companies that could provide raw materials and supplies to your organization. There are three companies that could be selected. You need to determine which of the three you will select as your supplier and present your recommendation and supporting rational to your immediate manager, as well as to his boss.

40. 2. You have been elected to represent your department on a special committee made up of individuals from different departments within the company. The purpose of the committee is to discuss and resolve several problems that are impacting your department and the other departments represented on the committee. You will have to present your views and opinions in a clear and forceful manner, defend them to the other committee members, and ultimately negotiate solutions with the other committee members.

or 4. You have been given the responsibility for evaluating a new piece of equipment that the work unit is considering purchasing. The equipment could significantly improve the overall productivity of the unit. You will need to assess current productivity, assess the potential impact of the new equipment, evaluate the cost of the proposed equipment relative to potential productivity increases, and submit a recommendation to your manager.

Scoring the Aspirer Test

In the Aspirer Test, each pair of statements included one statement that related to a managerial/supervisory activity, and one statement which related to a nonmanagerial/nonsupervisory activity. You were therefore being asked to choose between managerial/supervisory activities and nonmanagerial/nonsupervisory activities. As such, the test provided you with a direct measure of your preference for confronting managerial/supervisory challenges.

Before you score the test, review the 13 statements below, grouped by managerial/supervisory and nonmanagerial/nonsupervisory activities.

Managerial/Supervisory Activities

#2. You have been elected to represent your department on a special committee made up of individuals from different departments within the company. The purpose of the committee is to discuss and resolve several problems that are impacting your department and the other departments represented on the committee. You will have to present your views and opinions in a clear and forceful manner, defend them to the other committee members, and ultimately negotiate solutions with the other committee members.

#3. You have been asked by your manager to conduct a day-long training session with several newer employees in the work unit. The session involves explaining the company's employee benefits program. Conducting the session will require you to make several formal presentations to the group and facilitate several group discussion sessions with the employees.

#5. You have been assigned to handle a somewhat complicated project that the unit unexpectedly received. The project has a tight deadline, and you have been put in charge of two other staff members who will assist you with the project. You will be responsible for developing all timetables for the project, including detailed schedules for yourself and the two other staff members assigned to the project.

#6. You are responsible for training a new employee in the work unit. You will be responsible for reviewing her work, providing feedback to her regarding work she submits, and evaluating her general performance after she has been in the unit for two months.

#7. Two employees in the unit have had several significant arguments over the past two months, and there is considerable tension between them. One of the two employees comes to you and asks you to meet with the two of them to see if you can help mediate the situation.

#8. One of your employees, who reports directly to you, has been late in completing the last several assignments you gave him. This has created problems for the work unit. You must meet with the employee and tell him that this situation can no longer continue and that he must submit his assignments in a more timely manner.

#10. During the past month you have been studying different companies that could provide raw materials and supplies to your organization. There are three companies that could be selected. You need to determine which of the three you will select as your supplier and present your recommendation and supporting rational to your immediate manager, as well as to his boss.

#12. Your manager has asked that, for the next month, you work closely with a relatively new employee in the work unit. Thus far the employee has demonstrated less than adequate job performance. At the end of the month the employee will finish her probationary employment period, and your manager will want you to make a recommendation as to whether the employee should be retained or terminated.

Nonmanagerial/Nonsupervisory Activities

#1. You have been assigned a new project and given a deadline for completing it. You will be solely responsible for determining the different activities that need to be done, the order in which they will need to be done, and so on.

#4. You have been given the responsibility for evaluating a new piece of equipment that the work unit is considering purchasing. The equipment could significantly improve the overall productivity of the unit. You will need to assess current productivity, assess the potential impact of the new equipment, evaluate the cost of the proposed equipment relative to potential productivity increases, and submit a recommendation to your manager.

#9. You have been asked to develop a standardized procedure for the manner in which technical proposals are prepared. Once developed, the standards will be used by everyone in the work unit.

#11. You have been given the opportunity to attend a three-month training course that will enhance your technical skills. After attending the session, you will be solely responsible for doing the portions of any projects the work unit undertakes that involve this particular technology.

#13. You have an opportunity to take full responsibility for personally doing all sales presentations required of the work unit.

Now, to score the Aspirer Test, please do the following:

1. Go back to your responses to the 40 pairs and count the number of times you checked a managerial/supervisory activity, that is, statements 2, 3, 5, 6, 7, 8, 10, and 12. The sum can range from 0 to 40.
2. Write the sum in the space below.

My score on the Aspirer Test is _____ .

Calculating and Interpreting Your Aspirer mq

1. Write your score again here _____ .
2. Calculate your mq by dividing your score by 40, and then multiplying by 100. Place your answer directly below.*

$$\frac{\text{My total score}}{40} \times 100 = \underline{\hspace{2cm}} \text{ Aspirer mq.}$$

Interpretation of mq

An mq of at least 75 indicates satisfactory performance with respect to the attribute being measured. It essentially means that you earned at least 75 percent of the total possible score. This 75 percent level associated with satisfactory performance is based upon our collective experience with thousands of people taking managerial/supervisory attribute tests. As your mq approaches 100, it becomes more and more exceptional. If your mq is in the 90's, you would find yourself in approximately the top 10 percent of the test takers. With an mq in the 80's, this would place you in the top 30 percent of test takers, and an mq of 75 would mean you were in the top 50 percent of test takers. An mq of below 75 would put you in the bottom 50 percent of test takers.

Developmentally speaking, any mq of below 75 would indicate an attribute in need of development. This will be discussed in further detail in Chapter 9.

---

* Round off the result to the nearest whole number. Your mq can range from 0 to 100.

The Self-Developer

The Self-Developer demonstrates behaviors associated with a need to develop one's own abilities to a greater degree. The Self-Developer is one who practices skills, enrolls in courses, and looks for feedback from others who are in a position to give it. In other words, the Self-Developer typically strives for a higher level of performance in key areas with which he or she is concerned. Typically, Self-Developers are comfortable working on their skills either alone or with others, are generally well organized in regard to their time and how productively they use it, and are comfortable with negative as well as positive feedback.

Commitment to self-development is critical. You can't *depend* on others. Others can only assist you. You must be the main player in your own development. Self-development is an ongoing process; growth is never ending.

In this chapter you will be asked to review your attributes, in terms of your peaks and valleys, based upon the results of the tests you took in the previous chapters, and to identify three attributes most in need of development.

Next, you will be presented with almost 175 tips and strategies for enhancing your attributes. These are grouped according to the particular attribute. You will be asked to select the tips and strategies that are most appropriate for *you*, as you work on the attributes you have identified.

Identifying Attributes to be Developed

We will now have you record your mq's from Chapters 2 through 8 on the form below.

Attribute	mq
Administrator	_____
Analyzer	_____
Counselor	_____
Communicator	_____
Meeter	_____
Mentor	_____
Aspirer	_____

What attributes should I attempt to develop? In answering this question, list, at a minimum, your *three* lowest-scoring attributes. We recommend three to begin with, expanding to further attribute development as time permits. These three would generally include attributes on which you scored lower than 75. However, if you scored 75 or higher on *all* attributes, you would still want to choose the three lowest for developmental attention.

Looking at your mq's, select your three lowest attributes and list them on the form below.

Three Lowest Attributes

1. _____

2. _____

3. _____

These three attributes are the ones for which you will prepare specific developmental plans.

Identifying Developmental Strategies

In this section we describe different tips and strategies that will assist you in developing your different attributes. Many are applicable to individuals who are currently supervisors or managers; others to those who aspire to supervisory/managerial positions. Below are some suggestions for beginning, and continuing to build on, your developmental plans and strategies.

Guidelines

1. The best plans are written plans. Committing your developmental plans to writing is important. Use the Developmental Planning Forms which follow to develop your written plans.
2. As you review the different developmental tips and strategies listed for each attribute, bear in mind that many of the activities can be performed outside the work environment. Community organizations and programs are an excellent and "safe" environment for practicing and learning new abilities.
3. Most of the activities listed below are equally applicable to individuals currently in supervisory or managerial positions and to individuals who aspire to such positions. Although a given activity may refer to some form of direct interaction, view the actual activity broadly. It could involve someone other than the recipient of a formal direct report in a business setting.
4. Develop realistic goals and timetables. Development takes time. It is much better to list three or four developmental activities for a given attribute and follow through on them in a timely manner than to list an overly ambitious number of activities and ultimately do nothing because the task appears too imposing. Initially, limit your list to no more than four activities per attribute.

5. After developmental tips and strategies have been listed for each attribute, share the plan with someone whose opinions and skills you value. This may be the person to whom you currently report, a peer, or simply a close friend. Ask for feedback; for example, ask the person if the activities you listed reflect the attribute that needs development. Also, by sharing your plan with someone else, your own commitment to the plan will be increased.

6. Notice that for each developmental tip and strategy you list, the Development Planning Forms ask for a specific date on which you will review your progress on the activity. If you do not monitor your progress, little progress is likely to occur.

7. Development is an ongoing process. Once you master the activities you have listed for a given attribute, move on to others that will further enhance that attribute, or work on developing some other attributes. The goal is not simply to complete your initial development plans, but rather to look at your development, viewing it as an ongoing and never-ending process.

Developmental tips and strategies for each attribute begin on the following pages:

Developmental Planning Form

Name of Attribute: _____

Date Plan Was Prepared: _____

Developmental Tips/Strategies to Be Undertaken	Date Progress Is to Be Reviewed
1. _____	_____
2. _____	_____
3. _____	_____
4. _____	_____

Developmental Planning Form

Name of Attribute: _____

Date Plan Was Prepared: _____

Developmental Tips/Strategies to Be Undertaken	Date Progress Is to Be Reviewed
1. _____	_____
2. _____	_____
3. _____	_____
4. _____	_____

Developmental Planning Form

Name of Attribute: _____

Date Plan Was Prepared: _____

Developmental Tips/Strategies to Be Undertaken	Date Progress Is to Be Reviewed
1. _____	_____
2. _____	_____
3. _____	_____
4. _____	_____

ADMINISTRATOR

Structuring tasks for self or others, coordinating activities and resources, establishing work systems, and establishing group objectives.

- Assess how individual direct reports apply their time. Reassign job responsibilities or projects as necessary, to achieve a better balance of the work load.

- Keep a written record of assignments made. This record should include: a description of the assignment; the name of the person to whom work has been assigned; a description of milestones to be achieved along the way, along with planned interim completion dates; and a date for completion of the overall assignment.

or

If you are not currently a manager or supervisor, prepare such a record on each assignment delegated to you.

- When doing paperwork, determine both the relative importance and the relative urgency of each individual issue. Matters that are relatively unimportant and that are not urgent can usually be done by a direct report.

- When accepting or delegating an assignment, consider its impact on existing assignments or obligations. Keep a list of current assignments/obligations for yourself and require the same of direct reports.

or

If you are not currently a manager or supervisor, keep an up-to-date list of current assignments, with due dates and estimates of the time needed to complete them.

- Many excellent software programs on project management are available. Choose one and learn how to use it.

- Before conducting a meeting, determine what topics you will discuss. Rank these in order of importance and assign each a set amount of time for discussion. Keep discussions focused on the topic at hand, and make sure others are aware of the time expended.

- When undertaking or delegating an assignment, estimate the total amount of time the assignment should require. Upon completion, determine the actual amount of time expended.

- As with short-term job assignments, keep a summary list of all projects given to others. At a minimum, the list should include the name of the person responsible for the project, when it was assigned, and when it is to be completed.

- Keep a record of the problems that develop on each project. At completion, meet with direct reports to discuss how similar problems can be avoided on future projects.

or

If you are not currently a manager or supervisor, keep a record of your own projects, and initiate similar discussions on project problems with your supervisor.

- Maintain a daily "to do" list. Prioritize each task and work in order. Weekly and monthly lists are beneficial as well. Check off tasks as completed.

- Maintain a *personal* calendar for the year. Use it to schedule appointments, note important due dates, and so on.

- Maintain a *project* calendar for the year. Use it to plan and monitor critical completion dates and other critical matters.

- Record personal work activities during each hour. Continue this practice for a period of two to three weeks. At the end of that time, review the list and identify the types of activities that consume large portions of time. Then assess these activities to determine their relative importance. Know how time is actually spent.

- Require direct reports to keep a similar log of personal work activities. Then discuss the results as a group.

- When planning a project or task, anticipate problems. Review similar projects that went awry. Learn from earlier mistakes and take them into consideration when planning similar activities.

- Ask your supervisor for feedback on your administrative skills and specific suggestions for improvement.

- Many self-study programs and seminars are available on topics such as time management and how to develop organizing and planning skills. Ask your supervisor or training department for assistance in selecting a program.

- Set aside several hours each day for doing the more important or more difficult tasks. During this time, make sure others know that you prefer not to be disturbed, unless something important or urgent has developed.

Actively influencing the actions and thinking of others through effective delegation of work assignments and activities.

- Distribute work assignments evenly and fairly among direct reports by taking into account the amount of work each can handle and their personal preferences for certain types of assignments. Avoid giving the same direct report all the routine or unpleasant tasks simply because he or she performs them well or quickly. Also, avoid over-burdening highly skilled or motivated direct reports simply because they are willing to take on more work. Have all direct reports share in the work load as equally as possible.

- Assess how individual direct reports use their time. Reassign job responsibilities or projects as necessary in order to achieve a better balance of the work load.

- When delegating tasks or assignments to others, always specify expectations regarding the quality of the final product, as well as both interim and final deadlines for the task or assignment. Also, tell others you need to be notified well in advance if they cannot meet the agreed-upon deadline.

or

If you are not currently a manager or supervisor, always clarify deadlines and quality expectations at the time an assignment is given you. Also, periodically inform others about your progress on the assignment, and bring any problems to their attention immediately.

- When delegating assignments, capitalize on the performance strengths of each individual direct report. All direct reports won't be capable of doing all tasks equally well.

- Know the skills of each direct report. Prepare a list of each individual's special training or expertise. Include information about job-related interests. Use this list when delegating assignments, or when determining the developmental needs of individual staff members or the staff as a whole.

- When either delegating or undertaking an assignment, estimate the total amount of time the assignment should require. Upon completion, determine the actual amount of time expended.

- Require direct reports to keep a similar time log. Then discuss the results as a group.

- When appraising the performance of direct reports, include a measure of their project management or administrative skills. All planning and administrative responsibilities need not rest solely with the manager or supervisor.

Establishing follow-up and monitoring procedures to help ensure quality performance by self and others.

- Have direct reports develop written plans and timetables for major projects and assignments you delegate to them. Review plans and timetables with them, and assist with revision as necessary. Help with planning, but allow direct reports to do as much of the initial groundwork as possible. This will assist them in fully understanding the project more quickly.

or

If you are not currently a manager or supervisor, develop written plans and timetables for new assignments given you and review them with your supervisor.

- Set aside specific blocks of time each week to prepare plans for new undertakings and to review the status of existing assignments.

- Track incomplete work or missed deadlines for each direct report. Periodically review results with each individual. Also, summarize the information in group form, and periodically discuss results at group meetings.

- As with structuring tasks and establishing systems, maintain a *personal* calendar for follow-up and monitoring procedures. Use it to schedule appointments, note important due dates, and so on.

- Maintain a *project* calendar similar to the above. Use it to plan and monitor completion dates and other critical matters.

- Routinely meet with each individual direct report to review the status of his or her assignments. Check on timetables, and ask about any anticipated problems.

ANALYZER

Identifying, assimilating, and comprehending the critical elements of a situation by identifying alternative courses of action and evaluating salient factors and the elements essential to resolution of issues.

- Before finalizing important or complicated decisions, present your perceptions and ideas to someone whose judgment you value. Encourage them to take a "devil's advocate" role.

- Spend time assessing the causes of a problem *before* generating possible solutions. All too often action is directed at the symptoms of a problem rather than the actual causes. For example, overtime in a unit may be running very high and causing budget problems. But if the *cause* of the overtime problem (e.g., too few staff members, improper scheduling, poor coordination with other work units) is not accurately identified, correct problem-solving actions cannot be initiated.

- Assess problem solving plans and actions from different perspectives (i.e., financial implications, political implications, impact on other departments, etc.). Avoid looking at problems only from your own technical bias or operating responsibility.

- Seek advice and input from peers and managers who have experience and proven track records. It's unlikely that you are the only person to have experienced a particular problem.

- Ask your supervisor or manager to explain and discuss the thinking that went into significant decisions. Discuss the different options that were considered, reasons why particular options were eliminated, major reasons why the selected option was chosen, and so on.

- When assessing solutions to problems, look at potential risks or the downside potential of a particular course of action. Don't simply focus on possible positive outcomes.

- Keep a record of problems that develop on each project and assignment. Periodically review these records and look for trends. (Are problems attributable to a lack of communication, or to improper scheduling or planning?) Use these records to anticipate future problems on similar projects and assignments and to plan problem-solving strategies.

- Monitor and assess the impact of your decisions and remain flexible. As necessary, modify prior decisions, based on how you perceive the effectiveness of the implemented actions.

- When attempting to determine the cause of a problem, or when trying to evaluate possible courses of action, write down all pertinent information. Then review the information and decide whether any additional information should be obtained before final conclusions are drawn.

- Use group brainstorming sessions to generate a long list of possible solutions for a particular problem. Don't evaluate ideas until each has been fully explained and recorded. The purpose should be to develop as many ideas as possible. Evaluation of the ideas should be done later.

- Volunteer to serve on a special committee or task force made up of individuals from different departments, or on one whose members come from different disciplines. This is an excellent way to gain exposure to different perspectives on an issue or problem.

- When dealing with a large amount of detailed information, make the information as user friendly as possible. For example, mark or highlight important facts, and summarize numeric information into tables and graphs.

- If you are currently a supervisor or manager, make use of input from direct reports. When possible, enlist input in problem-solving sessions where additional ideas and strategies will be generated and where direct reports will have a greater sense of ownership in actions ultimately implemented.

- Consider the organizational climate and culture in implementing your problem-solving strategies. Strategies may be considered highly effective in one organization but not in another organization.

Using logical and sound judgment in the determination of appropriate courses of action, based on the facts available.

- When planning long-term assignments or projects, try to anticipate problems. Make a list of potential problems or obstacles and jot down a few contingency plans for each.

- Make use of others in diagnosing problems and generating solutions. "Group think" often yields the best solutions.

- In determining solutions to problems, generate a number of options. Then assess the merits and shortcomings of each. Avoid hasty decisions. Don't accept your first idea as the "only" course of action.

- As with identifying critical elements and courses of action, volunteer to serve on a special committee or task force made up of individuals from different departments, or on one whose members come from different disciplines. This is an excellent way to gain exposure to different perspectives on an issue or problem.

- Clearly define goals or objectives in behavioral terms; include quantifiable results and dates for accomplishment. It is difficult to assess the impact of a decision or an action if objectives are specified.

- Avoid inaction because of a problem's magnitude or complexity. If possible, break the problem down into its various component parts and deal with each separately. Also, bear in mind that while an "ideal" solution may not be readily available, actions that partially improve a situation are of significant value.

- If they are available, volunteer for rotational work assignments in different functional areas. The experience will broaden your perspective and increase your problem-solving skills.

- Keep abreast of new developments and thinking by reading trade journals and other professional publications that relate to your functional area and industry at large.

- Ask your supervisor or manager if you can accompany him or her to some higher-level meetings where higher-level problem solving will take place.

- Take advantage of training offered by your organization. Courses in problem solving, quality circles, quality control, and so on will assist you in further developing your analytical skills.

- Most people have a time of day during which they are most effective in dealing with complicated or creative matters. Use these "peak" periods for the majority of your problem-solving activities.

- Once you decide on a course of action, develop a written list of pro's and con's. Capturing your thoughts on paper, in addition to "thinking through" issues, will help identify factors that have been either overlooked or given inadequate weight in the decision-making process.

- Keep a list of significant problem-solving actions taken and the rationale for them. Periodically, review the list with your supervisor or manager and seek his or her feedback.

- Initiate actions to deal with problems, even if you are unable to define the problem precisely or generate possible solutions. Enlist the aid of your supervisor or manager. Don't allow problems to go unchecked. In addition to recognizing a problem, directing it to someone who can deal with it effectively is also part of the overall problem-solving process.

COUNSELOR

Responding sensitively to the needs and feelings of others, and giving constructive feedback to others.

- Commend others for positive performance, and explain why you viewed their performance as positive.

- Praise and acknowledge the efforts of others in front of others. However, provide feedback of a critical nature only in private.

- Avoid providing negative feedback or criticism to others until you are fully aware of all surrounding circumstances.

- When feasible, focus discussions on results, not people. For example, the statement, "Deadlines for the project weren't met; how can this be avoided in the future?" rather than "You didn't meet the deadlines for the project; what do you need to do differently in the future?" will lead to a more productive discussion and less defensiveness on the part of the employee.

- Feedback, of either a positive or critical nature, should be given promptly. Waiting weeks or months to discuss a performance issue lessens the effectiveness of the feedback.

- Feedback should be an ongoing and continuous process; not simply a once-or-twice-a-year event. Although formal appraisal sessions may occur infrequently, informal coaching and counseling to improve performance should be a part of everyday supervisory/managerial activities.

- When evaluating the performance of others, evaluate results and how the results were achieved. Avoid assuming that the way *you* would have personally done an assignment is the "best" or most effective method.

- Focus feedback on meaningful issues or problems. Everyone occasionally makes mistakes. It is unrealistic to expect perfection on every assignment.

- Feedback is most effective and best received when it is behaviorally specific. Discuss behaviors and results that actually occurred (or did not occur). Vague generalizations (e.g., "The report is poorly written"; "You need to be more sensitive in your interactions with others") are difficult for others to understand and usually lead to little behavioral change on the part of the employee.

- Keep a file for each employee. Periodically enter written comments regarding their performance and the feedback you have given them. This will help you identify performance trends and will be of great assistance in formal appraisal sessions. Typically, what is not recorded in writing is forgotten over time.

- For a two- or three-week period, record the number of times you provide performance feedback to others. Then review the record to determine the proportion of your feedback that was critical, relative to the proportion that was positive and encouraging. If a significant proportion of your feedback has been critical, strive for better balance. As a goal, praise others more often than you criticize them.

- Couple critical feedback with positive feedback. If you need to bring a problem to someone's attention, do so. But at the same time, point out some of your positive observations.

- Feedback and coaching are most effective when related to a specified goal, objective, standard, or criterion. When giving assignments, make sure the employee is fully aware of your expectations regarding the assignment.

- Before giving critical feedback on a significant issue, assess how *you or others* may have contributed to the problem (e.g., was adequate direction originally given the direct report, did I adequately monitor progress on the assignment?).

- Prepare for formal feedback sessions. List the performance issues to be discussed, behaviorally document the employee's performance in these areas, and formulate tentative lists of probable causes of problems and things that need to be done to improve performance in each area.

- Create opportunities for feedback to occur. Set up a procedure for reviewing each direct report's performance upon completion of each major assignment. Institute informal performance review sessions with each direct report on a quarterly basis.

- Avoid giving critical feedback when you are angry or annoyed with the individual in question.

- In deciding how to prevent a performance problem from occurring in the future, carefully assess the possible causes of the problem. Problems may be due to one or more factors, such as lack of skill or training, experience, motivation, and so on.

- Develop a list of performance issues that appear to affect a significant number of your direct reports. Then, in conjunction with your supervisor or manager, develop a plan of action for addressing the issues.

- Many excellent courses and seminars are commercially available for improving coaching and counseling skills. Ask your manager or training unit for assistance in locating an appropriate course.

- Follow up on performance discussions in which you have communicated to others a need for improvement. Monitor improvement and provide feedback accordingly.

Displaying an openness for others' views and opinions, as well as soliciting others' views and opinions.

- Make feedback a two-way process. After discussing a problem or issue with an employee, ask for his or her perception of the causes, of what can be done to improve, and so on. Avoid simply lecturing.

To the greatest extent possible, create a mutual problem-solving atmosphere.

- Solicit honest feedback from direct reports regarding your feedback and coaching skills. Ask them to provide you with examples of instances where your feedback has not been specific, where positive feedback was deserved but not offered, and so on.

- When conducting formal appraisals, seek input from others. Don't assume you have a complete picture of the employee's performance. Seek input from your manager and from other supervisory/management personnel with whom the employee may have interacted.

- When conducting a formal appraisal, seek input from the employee. Prior to the session, ask for a list of his or her accomplishments and significant performance incidents.

- Create an atmosphere that values open and constructive feedback. Ask direct reports for feedback on materials *you* personally develop. Rehearse a presentation with the group and ask for feedback. Don't be afraid to let them know about your own mistakes or errors.

- Seek input from others regarding how to best handle a particularly difficult performance issue. Your manager and other supervisors may have dealt with a similar performance issue or similar type of direct report in the past.

- Have direct reports review and critique each other's work before they submit it to you. Providing feedback is not the exclusive domain of the supervisor or manager.

- Ask your manager to observe you during a group feedback session at the end of a major project or assignment (e.g., review of a project with a group of direct reports upon project completion). Ask for his or her feedback regarding areas you could have been more specific about.

- Create an environment where "discussion" is routine. Establish a procedure for conducting informal, but routine, meetings with individual direct reports to discuss the status of projects. Specifically ask how you can be of assistance.

COMMUNICATOR

Expressing thoughts and ideas to others through verbal means, including using voice effectively, using effective nonverbal accompaniments, and organizing communications effectively.

- Attend to the nonverbal cues of listeners. If there are indications of disinterest or a lack of understanding, check to see that the listener understands what has been said.

- For meetings where you will be required to make a formal presentation, rehearse your presentation aloud. Rehearsals will add to your comfort level and enhance your ultimate delivery.

- When preparing an outline for a presentation, avoid developing a "script." Rehearse what you will cover and use the outline as an aid, not a crutch. Presentations that consist of the speaker simply "reading" to the audience are exceedingly boring.

- If overheads or slides are to be used for a presentation, ensure that the text can be easily read by all members of the audience. Overheads with typewriter-size text are next to impossible to read.

- If overheads or slides are to be used for a presentation, avoid constructing ones that contain paragraphs of text; brief statements are much more appealing visually. Also, avoid constructing a separate overhead for every point you want to make. Reserve overheads for points that may be difficult for the audience to understand or points that you want to emphasize.

- Lengthy monologues are seldom interesting, even in the context of a formal presentation. Preplan questions you can ask members of the audience or other activities that will "involve" the audience. Avoid lengthy periods where the audience is forced to simply sit and listen passively.

- When making presentations on complex or difficult topics, pause frequently to check for understanding and to invite questions.

- Seek feedback from others on your effectiveness. At the end of meetings, ask others to comment on your clarity, the length of time you spent on certain topics, and so on. When formal presentations are made, consider having the audience complete an evaluation form on the presentation.

- Tape-record meetings and presentations. Then assess your own delivery skills.

- If possible, videotape formal presentations. Then assess both your verbal and nonverbal delivery (also a highly effective strategy for rehearsals).

- Most all colleges and universities, as well as many other kinds of organizations, offer public speaking courses. In addition to teaching "technique," such courses offer a safe environment for overcoming stage fright.

- Avoid rambling, or providing too much detail. It is much better to have audiences ask for more information than to lose their attention due to overkill. Attempt to be brief and to the point.

- When giving instructions or providing information, ask listeners to summarize what you have said. This will ensure that the information you gave was clearly understood and will prevent problems due to misunderstandings.

- When receiving instructions or getting information, summarize what you have heard. This will ensure that you clearly understood the information and will prevent problems due to misunderstandings.

- When possible, do advance planning for important meetings or presentations. Develop an outline of the major points you want to present or discuss, and give thought to *how* you will explain or present the information.

- For meetings where you will be required to make a lengthy formal presentation, work from an outline. The outline should contain the major points to be presented, as well as the amount of time you plan to spend on each point.

- Distribute paper copies of overheads or slides to the audience before the presentation begins. Encourage listeners to make notes on the handout.

- When preparing for a presentation, develop a list of questions that might be asked by members of the audience. Preplan your responses to these questions.

- If you plan to make a given presentation more than once, note the questions that were asked that you had not anticipated. Then use this information to help refine your subsequent presentations.

- When preparing for a meeting or presentation, analyze the makeup of the audience—that is, how familiar are certain material and concepts; is the group diverse in experience, background, and interests? Then use your perceptions of the audience to gauge your level of detail, use of visual aids, amount of time spent on individual concepts, and so on.

Expressing thoughts and ideas to others through written means, including word choice, using appropriate grammar, and organizing communications effectively.

- Read aloud memos or reports you've prepared. If they don't "sound" clear, concise, or easy to follow, they won't "read" that way either. Use this technique to help you edit documents.

- Keep written sentences and paragraphs as short as possible. Although a three- or four-line sentence may be grammatically correct, it will make for difficult reading.

- Give thought to the visual impact of materials. Underline or "bold" important information; use "bullets" instead of sentences to draw attention to key points.

- Most all colleges and universities offer writing courses. Take advantage of them.

- Collect several pieces of your written work and submit them to your supervisor or manager. Ask him or her to review the documents and then meet with you to discuss how the documents could have been improved.

- Collect and study memos and reports you receive. Identify ineffective ones and rewrite them for practice.

- Avoid using highly technical jargon or uncommon words. A simple and unaffected writing style is more easily read and understood.

- Volunteer for assignments that will require you to use your writing skills. Practice is important for improvement.

- Keep reference materials, such as a dictionary, a grammar reference, and so on, handy when writing.

- Keep a record of any reports or memos that are returned for revision or about which others have questions. Look for trends in the materials and identify the most common cause of problems.

- When preparing memos or reports, try to write them several days in advance of distribution. Then reread and edit them a day or two later. Most people have difficulty critically reading and editing material they have prepared if the material is still "fresh" in their minds.

- When preparing a lengthy document or report, develop an outline before you begin to write. Doing so will help you determine the proper order for presenting various kinds of information.

- Avoid using memos as a substitute for a phone call or a face-to-face meeting.

- When preparing a lengthy report, draw up a two-page abstract of the report and include it at the front. An abstract essentially summarizes the key information contained in a report.

- Before distributing important documents, seek feedback from others. Ask for feedback on clarity, adequacy of information provided, order of presentation, and so on. Then make revisions accordingly.

- As is true with oral presentations, when preparing written material consider the background of the reader or readers. This will assist you in determining the appropriate level of detail needed, and other matters.

- When preparing important documents, allow adequate time for writing, editing, and rewriting. Time and effort are required to produce well-written documents.

MEETER

Encouraging others to participate and contribute in meetings by giving them opportunities to do so.

- When conducting group meetings, particularly with direct reports, allow members to voice their ideas and suggestions fully. Refrain from evaluating an idea or suggestion until it has been fully proposed and explained.

- When conducting group meetings, particularly with direct reports, refrain from being the first person to evaluate a proposed idea or suggestion. Instead, ask others for comments and reactions.

- When conducting group meetings, particularly with direct reports, encourage all group members to participate. If certain members appear reluctant to participate, ask them specific questions, to increase their level of participation.

- Ask open-ended questions.

- Reinforce others when they offer views and suggestions. Acknowledge their input, even though you may disagree.

- During group meetings, particularly with direct reports and peers, don't allow others to evaluate an idea until it has been fully presented and/or explained by the presenter.

- Before a major or complicated decision is finalized in a group meeting, briefly summarize the decision and supporting rationale. Then seek final agreement from the group at large.

- In some large group meetings, avoid wasting time by trying to get unanimous approval for every decision. In some instances, the amount of time spent trying to achieve consensus is not worth it.

- Encourage your manager to attend a group meeting you conduct and ask for his or her feedback on the meeting.

- Ask participants for feedback on meetings you conduct (e.g., was the meeting necessary, did you encourage open dialogue, were goals accomplished?).

Prioritizing the demands of meetings, establishing systematic means for achieving results, stating objectives, and clarifying group goals.

- When you are responsible for conducting group meetings, prepare a written agenda in advance. List goals and/or objectives that need to result from the meeting and key issues that need to be discussed. Distribute the agenda to others in advance of the meeting.

- Make notes during meetings. Keep track of key decisions made, their rationales, unresolved issues, follow-up actions planned, and so on. This is particularly important in group meetings where many different points of view may be expressed.

- When conducting meetings, particularly group meetings, determine how long the meeting should last. Monitor time during the meeting and attempt to stay within the limits you set.

- When conducting meetings with groups of direct reports or peers, have a pre-established starting time and begin promptly. Stragglers will quickly learn to be on time, and time will not be wasted.

- When meeting with direct reports, don't allow the meeting to be needlessly interrupted. Minimize interruptions due to personal calls or other matters that are not urgent or important.

- Avoid spending excessive time discussing issues that cannot be readily resolved. Learn to recognize issues that cannot be finalized without additional data gathering, that require approval or cooperation of others not present, and so on.

- Take time to personally prepare for meetings. Anticipate possible objections and obstacles, be ready with alternative strategies, and formulate initial points of view. Come prepared, regardless of your role in the meeting.

- Use visual aids to summarize information or to explain complicated information to others.

- Keep discussions focused on problems and issues. Avoid letting issues become "personalized" when conflict occurs among group members.

- Make audiotapes of several meetings you conduct. Listen to the tapes and assess areas where improvement would be beneficial.

MENTOR

Developing and nurturing the abilities and potential of other individuals, allowing them to grow to their maximum level of effectiveness.

- Avoid providing answers immediately to direct reports' questions. Instead, ask questions of them regarding their suggestions or ideas for handling issues. Stimulate others to think through issues before they ask for guidance.

- Make sure that others view you as approachable. Encourage others to approach you for assistance or advice.

- Involve more senior employees in the training and development of newer employees.

- Make challenging assignments to individuals. Be willing to take some risks for the benefit of others.

- Share "power" with others. For example, allow direct reports to chair meetings you convene, or ask for their input on significant decisions.

- Require all direct reports to maintain and continuously work on a developmental plan. Share yours with them and set an example.

- Stress performance improvement on an individual basis. Avoid creating an overly competitive environment where direct reports are constantly compared to one another.

- At least yearly, discuss with each direct report his or her long-range developmental plan. Attempt to provide some assignments during the course of the year that are consistent with the plan.

- Organize some form of social contact with employees outside the office.

- Actively recognize positive performance in others. Doing so not only provides motivation, but also develops self-confidence.

- When a performance failure occurs, help the direct report to assess the reasons for the failure in a nonthreatening manner. Stress the learning value of the experience.

- Actively acknowledge positive accomplishment. Avoid discussing how a project or task could have been even more successful.

- Take the time to discuss issues unrelated to work. Let direct reports know that you are interested in them as individuals, above and beyond their work-related contributions.

- Periodically meet with individual direct reports to discuss "how things are going." Let the direct report decide what he or she wants to discuss.

- Inform superiors of the outstanding accomplishments of others.

- Express confidence in a direct report's ability to perform a given activity.

- Emphasize and positively recognize examples of "teamwork" among direct reports.

ASPIRER

Striving always for new goals, always looking toward the future and for ways to improve position on the job or in life.

- Seek out opportunities to work jointly with others on major projects as well as other assignments.

- Offer opinions and views, and defend them when challenged.

- Take an active role in directing group activities; volunteer to make presentations to groups.

- Systematically schedule your own work activities, as well as those of others.

- Take ownership for others' activities and completion of tasks. Offer feedback on how the activities could have been more effective.

- Mediate conflicts involving others.

- Carefully analyze problems; base conclusions on the facts provided.

- Once decisions have been made, defend them with the facts.

- Take ownership for the completion of projects, and monitor the work of others relative to agreed-upon time lines.

- Persist in efforts despite obstacles or setbacks. Look for ways to work around problems before setting new goals or courses of action.

This chapter has provided you with the information and methods you need to begin to develop your seven other attributes. The alternatives are numerous. It is up to you to select them and make it happen.

Developing your attributes will be an ongoing process. If you do it carefully, you and your organization will profit.

CHAPTER 10

Your MQ

In this concluding chapter, we will have you calculate your overall MQ.

Your overall MQ, as we discussed earlier in the book, tells you your overall capability as a manager. It tells you how you stand relative to existing managers and supervisors. Said differently, it tells you how good you are, if you are presently a manager or supervisor, or how good you would be, if you would like to be a manager or supervisor, or even if you are just wondering about it. It gives you the one number that is in itself a summary statement of your capability.

Like the mq's (the managerial quotients for the seven attributes not including self-development), the MQ can range from 0 to 100. An MQ of at least 75 indicates satisfactory capability. It essentially means that you earned at least 75 percent of the total possible score. As your MQ approaches 100, it becomes more and more exceptional. If your MQ is in the 90's, you would find yourself in approximately the top 10 percent of the test takers. With an MQ in the 80's, this would place you in the top 30 percent of test takers, and an MQ of 75 would mean you were in the top 50 percent of test takers. An MQ of below 50 would put you in the bottom 50 percent of test takers.

Now, let us have you calculate your MQ.

Record your mq's from page 187 in Chapter 9 on the form on the next page.

Attribute	mq
Administrator	_____
Analyzer	_____
Counselor	_____
Communicator	_____
Meeter	_____
Mentor	_____
Aspirer	_____

Add up the seven mq's, divide by 7, and round off to the nearest whole number. This will give you your MQ. Write it in the space below.

My MQ is _____ .

This, then, is your MQ, and it represents your overall capability as a manager/supervisor. It is the one number that takes into account all of the various competency factors and attitudinal factors associated with the effective application of managerial/supervisory responsibilities. Refer back to the previous page, if necessary, to review what your MQ means.

In Conclusion

In this book we have shown you the attributes associated with being a manager/supervisor. We hope you have found it to be of value. For it to continue to be of value to you, remember these basic points:

- Your attribute mq's have allowed you to identify your own relative strengths and weaknesses.

- Your developmental plan will allow you to further develop the attributes that you have identified as being in need of enhancement.
- Your MQ allows you to have an appreciation of your overall capability as a manager/supervisor.

Finally, let us share some of our thoughts with you. When you are an effective manager/supervisor, rewards obviously follow, some of which may not always be apparent.

For example, the act of being a "giving" manager, a mentor, one who is *willing* to take the time to allow others to grow and feel good about themselves, is a reward in itself. It is one friend taking pleasure in the development of another; a parent helping a child mature into a contributing member of society. Most of all, it is helping someone be what he or she can be with no other reward greater than the gratification of seeing it happen.

So, you see, a high MQ can mean self-satisfaction, even pleasure, and bring meaning to your life and the lives of others; and with that, we close.